Guide to
Effective Military Writing

Guide to Effective Military Writing

3RD EDITION

William A. McIntosh

STACKPOLE
BOOKS

Copyright © 2003 by Stackpole Books

Published by
STACKPOLE BOOKS
5067 Ritter Road
Mechanicsburg, PA 17055-6921
www.stackpolebooks.com

Cover design by Wendy A. Reynolds

Printed in the United States of America

Third edition

10 9 8 7 6 5 4 3 2 1

Library of Congress Cataloging-in-Publication Data
McIntosh, William A.
     Guide to effective military writing / William A. McIntosh.—3rd ed.
        p. cm.
     Includes index.
     ISBN 0-8117-2779-3 (pbk. : alk. paper)
     1. United States—Armed Forces—Records and correspondence. 2. Military art and science—Authorship. 3. English language—Rhetoric.
I. Title.
UB163.M36 2003
808'.066355—dc21

                                                                           2003001676

Contents

Preface vii

Part I: *Guidelines for Military Writing* 1

1 *Writing in the Military* 3

2 *A Standard for Military Writing* 15

3 *When to Write* 17

4 *Substance* 27

5 *Organization* 33

6 *Style* 51

7 *Correctness* 71

8 *Military Formats* 83

9 *Briefings and Oral Presentation* 93

10 *General Formats* 97

11 *Argument* 107

12 *Editing Techniques* 115

Part II: *A Checklist of Grammar, Usage, and Mechanics* 125

Index 223

Preface

Language is dynamic and a direct reflection of the society it exists to support. The faster a given society moves, the more subject its language is to change. Our society runs on a fast track. During the last half of the twentieth century, the Cold War relentlessly impressed itself on much of what people heard and said. These days, though, if you mention Cold War to a generation growing up on computerese, media-speak, and MTV glitz, you might as well be talking about a snowball fight.

As changes in our language occur, the conventions governing the way we write—conventions of usage, style, and form, for example—also change. Over the last decade technology and mass communications have accelerated that evolutionary process. Usage that would have been unacceptable as few as ten years ago has become coin of the realm.

Case in point: "There's many people . . . " is an introductory phrase typical of hundreds—thousands—like it that appear in daily papers, news broadcasts, television programs, and in the mouths of millions who know better but use it anyway. No one seems to notice or mind. Do people who use such constructions know that "there's" means "there is"? Do those who hear it? Probably. And perhaps most of them would not say, "There is many people," because they know it is wrong, though far fewer would be able to identify it as an agreement error.

How many times in the last year or two have you looked at the list of beverages on a menu and seen "ice tea" or received an invitation to an "old fashion" picnic? More than once or twice, I suspect. Has anyone ever told you that we are living in a "doggie-dog world" or that she is about to "hone in on" this or that? Have you ever sat on a "Chip and Dale" love seat? Unlikely, unless you're a chipmunk. "A person needs to take care of their health" is a statement that might well have referred to a Siamese twin a generation ago; nowadays a tongue-in-cheek remark of that sort is as politically incorrect for its insensitivity as the failure to use the gender-neutral language. Early on, gender-neutral usage of the last example was, quite simply, incorrect, but its social force has made it, first in speech and then in print, ubiquitous nonetheless. And its ubiquity is rapidly qualifying it as acceptable.

In the first edition of this book, I tried to dodge that particular grammatical bullet by assigning a gender to the hypothetical unisex "person." That way, I thought, I could say, "A sailor needs to practice her spelling," or "A soldier should consult his dictionary," without violating the very rules I was urging readers to follow. One of my reviewers criticized this approach, asserting that such variations were distracting and made the book hard to use.

As I recall, my critic took me to task for bowing to political correctness and urged me to abandon my flip-flopping solution. Fifteen years ago, my editors might have let me get away with saying, "A person needs to practice *his* spelling," but the second edition did not appear for another eight years, during which time more and more women entered military service. Some of them, I suppose, had occasion to consult, if not buy, the first edition of the book, and if I avoided irking some of them with "sexist language," I am glad.

In preparing the second edition, I considered the criticism of the first and responded to some of it. Frankly, I do not remember precisely how I tap-danced around the person/his/her problem that time around, but that is beside the point.

During the eight years between this book's second and third editions, changes in usage have occurred so rapidly as to have all but mooted the issue. (I say *all but* mooted because I still have a hard time surrendering the grammatical point. A person does not need to watch *their* p's and q's, dog-gone it, but instead *his* p's and q's or *her* p's and q's.) But as I argue in the text, there is a point where that kind of self-righteous scrupulosity becomes at best precious and at worst counterproductive.

Whatever the changes in our language and the rules for using it, you must still know how to write effectively and—insofar as our society will countenance it—correctly. The people who read your work have a right to expect good writing; that is, writing that is both *effective* and *correct*. Your superiors, if they are doing their jobs, will insist that you produce it. The reasons for that are basic enough. As a matter of duty, you are *supposed* (not "suppose") to, so get *used* (not "use") to the obligation of having to write well. The requirement is more than a matter of form for its own sake.

Good writing saves time, money, and materiel. More important, it saves lives. It ennobles the professions, distinguishes great leaders, and advances careers. The military has a traditional commitment to good writing. Over the seasons, local and unilateral programs to promote it have been legion. Most, alas, have been failures as well. Many reasons for those failures might be offered, but none would come closer to the mark than the one having to do with definition of terms.

To say it another way: Everyone knows what good writing is not, but not everyone can agree on what it is. This book does not presume to change all that; what it does do, however, is suggest a utilitarian compromise.

Few would argue that Shakespeare could not write well; in fact, *King Henry V* has lines in it that would make any military writer wildly jealous. But much of the play's language, however wonderful, has limited applicability to the armed forces of today.

On the other hand, a good deal of the military prose we read every day has no more applicability to our immediate situations than Shakespeare's does—and considerably less of its charm, elegance, and energy. In an ultimate sense, though, both examples amount to bad writing. Why? They do not, in the modern military context, communicate efficiently.

According to Shakespeare's countryman George Bernard Shaw, the acid-tongued dramatist, "There are only two qualities in the world: efficiency and inefficiency; and only two sorts of people: the efficient and the inefficient." Pressing Shaw's point, one might postulate two kinds of communication as well.

Writing that communicates efficiently is, by operational definition, good. But that's only half the equation. The other—and here's where Shakespeare carries the day in any context—has to do with grammar and usage. Not always, but as a general rule, effective communication must be grammatically correct, must follow the conventions of effective usage.

Again, why? Simply because an incorrect presentation distracts readers to such an extent that their concern focuses on the error rather than on the text. And that's not efficient.

Efficient communication depends not only on correct grammar and usage but also on the precise, economical, and appropriate use of words, all of which must be present against the context of the age in and for which it is produced.

For Renaissance England, Shakespeare produced good writing; for posterity, he produced great literature. Nevertheless, without considerable changes in style, he wouldn't last long, even on a low-level staff. In military circles today, good writing can have only one definition: effective communication.

Giving genius its due, we might confidently suppose that Shakespeare could come to terms pretty quickly with the repertoire of defense establishment forms and formats and with the techniques of producing good writing. Without stretching the point, we might even suppose he would do so intuitively. And it seems a good bet to suppose that Shaw would as well.

Other writers, however, might like a guide; hence, this book.

PART I

Guidelines
for Military Writing

1

Writing in the Military

The military is an active, fast-moving profession, and as such it would seem to have little need or time for the written word. But anyone who's been around the service for more than an afternoon knows better. The armed services, like other branches of government, appear almost obsessed with writing—and not just writing, but W R I T I N G prepared by one or more writers, coordinated and staffed by even more people, and reproduced by someone sitting at the keyboard of a computer loaded with spell check, grammar check, and a range of supporting applications that make it visually stunning.

Writing, however vital, pointless, worthwhile, self-serving, useful, wasteful, mission essential, mindlessly bureaucratic, urgent, or silly, is nevertheless a fact of military life. Perhaps the intense activity and transience of the profession demand the sense of stability and permanence that the written word transmits merely on the strength of its physical existence, if not in actual print, then at the very least somewhere on a zip drive or as an e-mail attachment.

Certainly the military needs records. What it doesn't need are the tons of paper and storage discs that get put into the system virtually every hour of every day. Need them or not, though, millions of documents make their way onto ships, into foxholes, aboard aircraft, into personal computers, and across desks around the world with horrifying regularity.

Whether things should be that way, that's the way they are. The upshot of this situation is that commanders and managers at all levels find themselves about to go under in a river of writing flowing into their actual and virtual inboxes boxes and spilling over their desks and computer monitors into bulging briefcases and smoking laptops at the end of the working day. Considerable energy, time, and effort go into reading all that stuff. In consequence, other important things don't get done, the boss gets harried and eventually hard to live with, and your own life takes a decided turn for the worse.

Now, if you think you're going to change any of that on a grand scale, guess again. Writing, and lots of it, is as basic to the armed forces as webbing or ammunition. People in leadership and managerial positions will always need to deal with a certain amount of writing. That's built into the system. In the main, you can do very little to affect the volume of what comes through their offices on paper or online, but you can do a great deal to affect its quality.

This book gives some fairly specific suggestions and techniques that can help you become an effective military writer. If you take them to heart, you will change the way you write. But before you change the way you write, you must change the way you think about writing.

The balance of this chapter deals with eight rules that will help you do that. Learning to live by them may be difficult. Don't despair. If all eight seem out of the question, grab hold of the one that bothers you the least. Commit yourself to the extent that you consciously follow it until you no longer need to make a special effort to do so. Once you get to that point, come back to this chapter and pick another rule.

Chances are that many of these rules will seem to make sense. That means you're already ahead of the game. Once you come to terms with the attitudes they represent, you'll rapidly be able to take advantage of the techniques this book proposes. Working toward that end, let's look at your responsibilities as a military writer.

THE WRITER'S RESPONSIBILITIES

Given the speed and volume of writing in the military, what can you do to improve the situation? For starters, try doing nothing that will make things worse. Specifically, you must resist the urge to write when writing isn't absolutely necessary. The basic rule every military writer ought to live by is this: *I will write only when I must.*

Now, a rule such as that runs against the military grain. Traditionally the services have associated a completed document with productivity: We must have done *something* or else we couldn't have written about it, right? Wrong. Plenty of stuff gets written that not only is not productive but actually is downright counterproductive. How about the daily bulletin notice that directs people to stay off grass already surrounded by a fence ten feet high? If that seems silly, it's only because it is.

Redundancy also gets in the way of productivity. In terms of tone and intent, this piece may have a familiar ring to it:

> Attached is your authorization to undertake official travel on behalf of the United States Government. It goes without saying that your expenditures while traveling should be those of a prudent person and that, upon return, your claim for reimbursement of those expenditures should be scrupulously accurate. To that end, the Finance and Accounting Office will review claims for reimbursement.

The writer of that annoying and utterly redundant passage is right about one thing: It goes without saying! Department of Defense Form 1351-2 comes to the same point memorably and without much equivocation:

> There are severe criminal and civil penalties for knowingly submitting a false, fictitious, or fraudulent claim (U.S. Code, Title 18, Sections 287 and 1001, and Title 31, Section 3729).

Of course there are times when it may be appropriate to state the obvious. But beating an issue to death doesn't do much for anybody. Nor does it make a whole lot of sense to write things down simply as a hedge against being blamed for a foul-up. The author of the first passage could have come to the point a lot more directly by saying: Don't cheat on your travel claims. The form makes clear that cheaters who get caught will get hammered. Given the penalties, perhaps anything else, even if it comes to the point quickly, may not be necessary.

When you do decide to write, write with single-minded dedication to the reader's understanding of what you have written. That leads to the second rule a military writer ought to live by: *I will write so my reader can understand what I am saying.*

Whether a reader understands what you have written depends on several significant variables. A few of them—your reader's native intelligence, experience, and prior knowledge of the subject—are beyond your control. The other variables—substance, organization, style, and correctness—are yours to command. And in fact, you can probably shape your writing to influence even those variables you don't control.

For instance, if your reader knows more than you do about the material you're writing on, you must pay particular attention to substance. If she's especially intelligent, then you have to take that into account as well. The point is, you have a lot to work with, and you will be able to use all of it effectively if you maintain an unswerving commitment to writing things that your reader can understand.

In addition to writing only when it's necessary and with total commitment to having your writing understood, you have a third responsibility: *I will not waste my reader's time.* By following the first two rules, you will automatically have fewer ways to violate this one.

Chapter 6 deals with style in some detail. At this point, suffice it to say that style and time have a close relationship. It's a relationship you must keep pretty clearly in mind if you hope to use your reader's time efficiently. If by now that isn't your hope, then you've missed the point altogether.

THE WRITER'S EGO

Some people like to write. For them it's an easy process. They understand words and the way they work together. They have fun using them to get things done. Such people seek opportunities to get their ideas down on paper. It doesn't take them long, and they invariably enjoy themselves while they're doing it. The mechanics of usage and grammar rarely seem to bother them, and spelling, most of the time, is a snap. They usually write without deletions and manage to crank their stuff out at a prodigious rate.

Others hate to write. For them writing is an agony. They know what words are and that they work together in complex and mysterious ways. Seldom can they identify those ways, and even less frequently can they use words to get things done. People of this sort despise the idea of putting their thoughts on paper, and they write with the utmost reluctance. They have no confidence in their knowledge of English usage or grammar. Spelling has always been one of their problems. Their writing implements vary widely. At any given time several wads of crumpled paper lie about their desks. They work slowly and fill their pages with arrows, scratch-overs, blotches—almost anything but coherently arranged words—or they sit in front of computer monitors looking at the few tortured sentences they have reluctantly allowed to survive.

Both kinds of people have one thing in common. At some point during the writing process, however easy or vexing, nearly all will come up with something that they think is all right. Or still more likely, they'll begin to think it's really pretty good—so good, in fact, that the thought of anyone tampering with it becomes painful, and the prospect of getting rid of it seems almost unbearable.

Sometimes, though, a passage of that sort can cause more problems than it solves. It might have very little to do with the issue that needs to be addressed. Or it might be too long. Worse yet, in reality it might not be such a work of art after all. But how tempting, especially if the passage was tough to write in the first place, to retain it at all costs, to include it simply because it's too good to get rid of. Don't give in to that temptation!

It's one thing for a poet to refuse to eliminate good lines that don't really work (though invariably a good poet will eliminate them), but military writers aren't in the business of composing poetry. Holding on to things that get in the way of effective communication represents a terrible kind of egotism, one that's as natural as it is deadly. Anyone who writes anything needs to guard against it.

Forcing yourself to throw out something you *know* is good takes real self-discipline. Quite simply, you have to be a little hard on yourself in the interest of efficient mission accomplishment, thus the fourth rule: *I will not preserve any of my material that might impede effective communication.*

THE WRITER'S FEELINGS

Most of us, at one time or another, have made mathematical errors. Some are more serious than others. But even when those of a very serious nature are discovered and brought to our attention (failing marks on an examination, overdraft notices from the bank), we do not take it personally. Sure, nobody likes to make a mistake, but in erring mathematically we rarely have much of the inner person at stake. Not so with words.

When we write, we are at our most vulnerable. In writing we necessarily discover and reveal to others parts of the self that we usually try very hard to protect. When someone judges our writing, it seems he is judging us—and not merely the thinking part of us, but the feeling part as well. People in the military, if the stereotype can be believed, shouldn't be affected by that sort of thing.

Precisely because they shouldn't be affected by such criticism, military writers tend to be particularly reluctant to receive it and even more reluctant to respond to it. Surely a John Wayne wouldn't let any of that bother him, so what's wrong with us that we can't shake it off? Nothing whatsoever. Few things we do are as personal as writing. That some of our writing happens to get done on the job doesn't change that.

Besides, a John Wayne *would* feel that way. Writing, no matter how uninspired or uninspiring, is a creative act. People don't like it when the things they create come under attack. Even slight criticism in the form of faint praise puts us on the defensive. And if what's getting criticized involved a lot of hard work, we can become almost intransigent in the face of any negative reaction to it.

None of that changes a thing. This isn't a book concerned with transactional analysis. Maybe you're OK; maybe you aren't. Or maybe your boss isn't. In any case, you still must write from time to time, and what you write will be subject to critical scrutiny.

Recognizing that your ego—and by extension your feelings—plays a large part in the writing process may help you get on with it a little easier. And if your writing doesn't come easier, at least you ought to be able to respond somewhat more objectively to any criticism it may receive.

Fixing the way you write is a lot easier than fixing the way you are. Most of the time your reader will be concerned with the way you write. Accept that, and even in a less-than-perfect world, you can get about the business of correcting your writing without having to waste the time and psychic energy all of us use passively hating (or actively plotting ways to get even with) the so-and-so who has attacked us. The rule? *I will not confuse criticism of my writing with criticism of me.*

CONTROLLING THE PROTECTIVE INSTINCT

One of the irksome things about clichés is that they are often true. How many times have you heard "If you don't take care of yourself, nobody will"? Plenty of military writers seem to take it as gospel. And they respond to it as if it really were. Thus acres of forests and untold gigabytes disappear each day for writers "taking care of themselves."

This kind of "protectionism" takes many forms. One is the memorandum for record. Now, some memoranda of that sort have critical value because they make up the body of institutional knowledge for organizations served by a transient staff. The military is one of those organizations. Can you imagine how difficult it would be to orchestrate a recurring training exercise without something to fall back on? How much ammunition should you order? What about fuel stocks? Another dozen questions would only scratch the surface. A memorandum recording those questions and their answers is not only legitimate but also almost essential.

The kinds of memoranda that have no real place are the ones that exist merely to protect the writer. Paradoxically, in tough situations they don't offer much protection at all. Suppose you have to scrub ten of ten scheduled flights because of maintenance deficiencies. Will the wing commander be content with a memorandum for record explaining that just last week you made a point of stressing materiel readiness with the maintenance crews? Probably not. So why write it? Instead, spend the time you save by not writing the memorandum supervising the maintenance of the aircraft that need it. Your commander wants the missions to occur as scheduled, not a piece of paper that attempts to show how hard you tried.

The point is, all the memoranda in the world won't provide much in the way of protection if things get really bad. And if they don't, there's no basis at all for such documents. Either way, they haven't got any real use. The mind-set that brings them into being is ultimately responsible for creating a good deal of confusion in all the services.

That confusion manifests itself in a lot of ways—the double standard that gets applied to reading and observing regulations, to name one. By definition, regulations demand adherence from those governed by them. Most servicemembers quickly learn, though, that two kinds of regulations exist: those they need to obey and those they can ignore. That distinction in day-to-day operations isn't confusing at all. It becomes confusing only when someone in authority decides to enforce a regulation that has been routinely violated for years. Even after such a "tightening up," if left alone for very long, that same regulation will quickly reclaim its place on the list called "regulations to ignore."

If all that seems to imply something about leadership, it is because writing and leadership have a fairly close relationship. But that's a subject for another book. The point here is this: If a regulation isn't important enough to enforce, it ought not to be written in the first place.

Memoranda, regulations, and directives that exist to show, after some disaster, that their writer was not at fault should not be written. In a way, the impulse to do that kind of writing is analogous to the purchase of term life insurance. Term life insurance makes good sense in some circumstances, but in buying it most of us show some restraint. Why? First, it costs money; second, if we don't die we'll have nothing to show for it. As a rule, people don't carry several million dollars' worth of term life insurance.

Writing, on the other hand, is "free." Consequently, we are frequently tempted to "over insure." However, in a military context, where production, processing, and storage costs all have to be absorbed by the system, there's nothing free about it. It's a luxury no one can afford.

Here's the acid test: Ask whether your writing is directed toward mission accomplishment or keeping yourself out of trouble. In most cases, if your first concern is accomplishing the mission, you won't get in trouble anyway. It would be naive to urge you never to write solely to protect yourself. Sometimes you must in order to survive in a complicated and demanding system. You can keep yourself honest most of the time, though, if you follow this rule: *I will keep my organization's mission at the heart of what I write.*

WRITING FOR SOMEONE ELSE'S SIGNATURE

One thing people in military service understand is the rank structure and their relative positions within it. In some ways, living in a system so rigidly structured is a snap. Your authority and obligations are dictated by statute. Rank and situation fundamentally determine the way you are going to act.

Every now and then, however, something can happen to throw that relatively clear-cut system out of joint—your assignment as an action writer or as a staffer, for instance. Whether such an assignment turns out to be great, merely all right, or hellish depends, in no small measure, on your immediate supervisor. It also depends on you and your ability to engage in a bit of role playing.

That means you're going to have to violate, in your head anyway, the relatively comfortable boundaries of the military hierarchy. In short, you need to get outside of yourself and assume the persona of the person who will ultimately sign your work. That's tough to do if you happen to be a major writing for a lieutenant general. Having a third party between the two of you makes this process even more complex.

Recognize the inevitability of a third party, build it into your role-playing equation as a constant, and get on with the business of stepping out of character. By putting on the face of the would-be signer, you will find yourself taking on her "voice" as well. And you will also find yourself thinking on an altogether different level.

The degree of success you have as a writer for someone else's signature will depend—and this point is critical—on how well you assume a persona that satisfies the intended signer's self-image. That means you must adopt a voice that portrays this person not necessarily the way he appears to you, but rather the way he *thinks* he appears. Reality probably exists somewhere between those two extremes. Curiously enough, your finished product will come pretty close to it.

Early on you need to come to terms with the third party (or parties) between you and the person whose signature you're writing for. You also need to come to terms with your own inhibitions. In both cases, you've got to do a little selling. The third party will likely have some of the same inhibitions you have. He or she may oppose what could be taken as an attempt to usurp something you haven't earned. Should things sort out that way, you'll simply have to muddle along as best you can.

That may mean having the courage, your supervisor's reservations notwithstanding, to go ahead and chance the role playing. If your results are good, nobody will complain; if they aren't, you won't have lost anything by having tried an approach that generally works pretty well. By the way, it would be foolish to expect this sort of thing to be a smashing success the first couple of times you try it. Like anything else, it will take a bit of patience and practice to master.

In time, this somewhat unnatural process will begin to serve you well. Dramatists and novelists make careers of doing fundamentally the same thing, so it's not exactly a new discovery. And it does work. When writing for the signature of someone else, insofar as the relationship between you and a third party will allow you to, hold fast to this rule: *I will write consciously using the voice and tone of the person whose signature will appear on my work.*

PRIORITIES AND FOCUS

Quite simply, if you can't set priorities and maintain focus, the writing requirements that come your way will bury you—that's after all the stuff you're confronted with that isn't required has already buried you. The first edition of this book hit the streets almost twenty years ago. Since then, the technology and protocols of military communications have changed radically, even though the basics have stayed essentially the same. Despite the changes, the lessons of this book are as applicable today as they were two decades ago. But you won't be able to implement them unless you set priorities and maintain your focus. Computers make doing that both easy and hard. They are virtually everywhere in the military, to say nothing of our personal lives. Because they are, the way in which, we communicate is in constant flux to take advantage of them and their expanding capabilities.

E-mail is an obvious case in point. Military communicators love it. Who can blame them? The ability to communicate with and send files to dozens—even thousands—at the click of a mouse is seductive. One might even say deadly. People are going to do to you what they will. By the same token, you will do to others as you will, too. I'm not about to climb on a soapbox decrying junk mail, particularly when one person's junk is another's proverbial treasure. I will, however, go so far as to say this: If you haven't contrived a way to manage e-mail's power, you have no hope of doing what you must as an effective communicator.

E-mail, like most anything else, is both a liberator and a tyrant. On the one hand, it saves time, money, and energy; on the other, it wastes time, money, and energy. Chances are you may have already recognized all that and figured out how to avoid some of the pitfalls. If you're lucky, the way you use and respond to e-mail is governed by some sort of SOP; if not, you ought to do everything you can to get one in place. That subject, too, is beyond the scope of this book.

Having raised it, however, I am reluctant to walk away from it without at least suggesting that if you use e-mail as a primary or secondary means of communicating, discipline yourself to stay away from your inbox until your own projects are off the screen. It's a matter of simple physics, really.

If you have a container with so much capacity, hundreds of grapes, and a half-dozen watermelons, what are you going to put in it first? If you fill it with grapes, most of the watermelons won't fit, which means they'll rot in place, and the one or two that do fit will squash the grapes underneath them. Instead, fill it with watermelons, and then start dropping the grapes in as time permits. They'll find their own place in the container. By doing that, you will have loaded watermelons before they spoiled and moved out a surprising number of grapes. Odds are that the ones left behind don't matter, and if they do, they'll be there tomorrow because grapes left long enough become raisins. E-mail will kill you.

General announcements, jokes, training schedules, football pools, action papers, duty rosters, and dozens of other things will turn up in your virtual inbox box each day. Figure out a way to distinguish the watermelons from the grapes, and then, if your time and energy allow, go back and sort through the grapes to see which ones you want to dump out of hand. The last rule? *I will set priorities and maintain my focus in responding to them.*

SUMMARY

If a single concern unites all the issues this chapter addresses, that concern is time. On the job, everything is a function of it. Another of those maddeningly demonstrable clichés—Time is money—comes directly to the point. As hinted at earlier, better writing won't reduce the amount of stuff that gets written. But it will certainly improve its quality. That means reduced reading time for each well-written document, increased efficiency, and better value for the dollars supporting the whole process. To that broad end, here are the eight rules for the military writer:

1. I will write only when I must.
2. I will write so my reader can understand what I am saying.
3. I will not waste my reader's time.
4. I will not preserve any of my material that might impede effective communication.
5. I will not confuse criticism of my writing with criticism of me.

6. I will keep my organization's mission at the heart of what I write.
7. I will write consciously using the voice and tone of the person whose signature will appear on my work.
8. I will set priorities and maintain my focus in responding to them.

2

A Standard
for Military Writing

For centuries, and my guess is for considerably longer, military and naval leaders have fretted themselves and their subordinates about writing. But for all the heat that their worrying has generated, it was not until relatively recently that much light began to materialize. During the 1970s and 1980s, the services redoubled their efforts to improve the dreary state of military prose, and by the late eighties most military schools had put a formal writing component in the curriculum. If approaches to the teaching of writing varied from service to service and school to school, a common standard for military writing emerged and remains in place today: *Good military writing, by definition, can be understood in a single, rapid reading.* A standard of that sort clearly favors the reader.

WHAT THE STANDARD MEANS TO WRITERS

The bias of a reader-friendly standard makes all the sense in the world in light of such issues as time and volume. It doesn't matter who gets asked, what uniforms they wear, or the kinds of billets they fill: Commanders and managers at all levels point repeatedly to the crippling demand writing puts on them. The written word chases them around the office, follows them home, saps their energy, and diverts their attention from other things that need it. In short, it rules many of their days (and nights) and brings only modest return against great investments of time, effort, and energy.

Too often the commander has to read with the intensity of a textual scholar examining an ancient manuscript merely to discover what a particular document is about. Occasionally he or she must rewrite entire documents simply because they are beyond simple editorial repair. When that happens, everyone loses. Commanders are meant to command; managers are meant to manage; people who write to or for them are meant to assist them in those functions.

The obvious way they can do that is by giving them good stuff to read. If things were intended to play out in any other way, the standard would serve the writer instead of the reader. It doesn't!

The writer who provides a document that cannot be understood even as it is being read is a substandard writer. The burden of producing a usable document is exactly where it ought to be: on the writer. Grammar must be generally correct as well. Grammatical errors prevent rapid reading. Why? They force the reader into an editorial role, and editing takes time.

General correctness, then, is the writer's responsibility, as are substance, organization, and style. Competence in all four areas is a must for writing that can be understood in one quick reading, which is the goal toward which every military writer must strive. If you don't feel confident in your ability to produce that kind of writing, you came to the right book.

Subsequent chapters will treat each of the four areas you need to master in order to measure up consistently to this standard. For now, make up your mind that you're going to measure up. In the next chapter, you can begin to come to grips with how.

3

When to Write

Dealing with the question of *when* to write is rarely easy, though chapter 1 gives a stock answer to it in the form of rule 1: I will write only when I must. Fair enough, but what does that really mean? For starters, you must write when your boss tells you to. Now, you do have an obligation to dissuade him if you believe that what you have been asked to write is not in fact necessary. That obligation, though, does not extend to disemboweling yourself with a number 2 pencil or punching your head through a computer monitor to make your point. Professional suicide won't solve a thing.

Instead, it will almost certainly lead to another kind of writing—about you rather than by you. If, however, you can discourage your superiors from adding to the billions of written words in the system, by all means do; if not, then just make sure that what you do end up writing is written as well as it can be.

Many times—perhaps most of the time—the choice of whether to write will be up to you rather than your boss. Given that, let's return to the matter of when you must write. In the final analysis, you must write when you have no alternatives to writing.

ALTERNATIVES TO WRITING

In a military context there are three generally accepted ways to communicate: face-to-face conversation, radio or telephone, and writing, which, of course, includes such things as e-mail. Without question, face-to-face conversation is quickest, cheapest, most direct, and least likely to be misunderstood. For all of that, though, it isn't as effective as we might expect. In face-to-face conversation, only some 80 percent of a given communication is understood in the way the person sending it intends. In face-to-face conversation we have five elements (see Figure 1).

Elements of Face-to-Face Conversation

1. **Words**
2. **Opportunity to ask questions**
3. **Feedback**
4. **Facial expression**
5. **Body language**

Figure 1.

Taken together, those elements of face-to-face conversation promise that most of what gets said will be understood. When using the radio or telephone, we do less well. No more than about 60 percent of the transmission gets understood. And sometimes the success rate is considerably lower, depending on such variables as equipment, distance, and weather.

You may recall a party game called "Telephone." For example, a group of kids sit in a circle facing out, with their backs to its center. Someone receives a piece of paper with a phrase written on it. That person whispers the phrase to whoever is sitting to the right; the new person, in turn, whispers it to the next person in the circle; and so on. When the message at last gets back to the person who started it, the contrast between what went out and what came back is usually pretty remarkable.

In the context of a party, that sort of thing can be great fun, but on the job, it can have disastrous consequences. Using the telephone has the same drawbacks that the game has. Because in the game everyone faces to the outside of the circle, both facial expression and body language count for very little. When using the telephone or radio, we find that they count for nothing at all. Rather, we must rely on the four elements shown in Figure 2.

It is tempting to argue that the conventions and procedures people follow when using the radio make the rate of understanding even lower than 60 percent. Either way, losing 40 percent of the message makes the case for doing business in person a fairly strong one. Facial expression and body language are the things that do the most to promote understanding; they are the things that make face-to-face conversation so much more effective than conversation over the telephone or radio.

Elements of Radio or Telephone Conversation

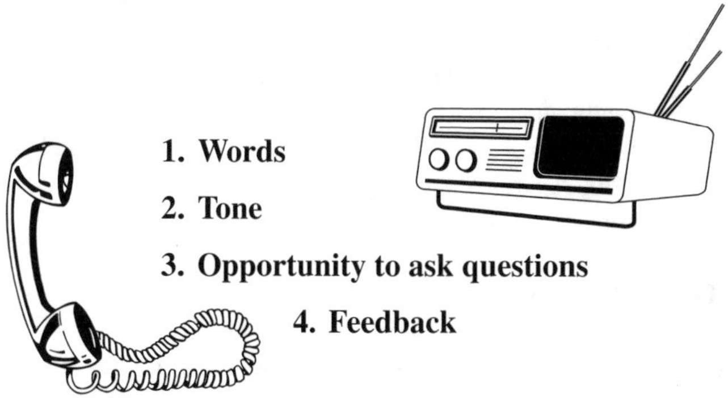

1. Words
2. Tone
3. Opportunity to ask questions
   4. Feedback

Figure 2.

Similarly, remove the opportunity to ask questions and the feedback that the telephone and radio give us, and we're left with the basic elements of written communication (see Figure 3).

The most we can realistically hope for from those who read what we write is a rate of understanding of around 40 percent. What that means is that in written communication (including e-mail), less than half of what we put down is likely to be understood by those who read it.

Whether you accept all these figures as correct—and there is plenty of evidence to show that they are—one thing should be obvious: Writing is the *least* effective means of communication available to us. Something else also ought to be obvious: When you have a choice, face-to-face conversation

Elements of Written Communication

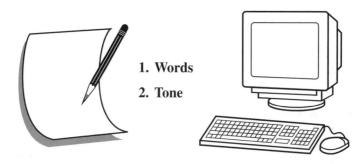

1. Words
2. Tone

Figure 3.

is the best alternative to writing. It usually doesn't require special equipment or a precise set of conventions to follow. And, clearly, it offers you the best chance of understanding and being understood.

Telephone and radio, in that order, are your second and third alternatives. Another advantage they share with face-to-face communication is their speed. Writing takes time, sometimes quite a lot of time, and you don't always have a lot to spare. And even if time were not an issue, it just doesn't make sense to opt for ineffectiveness.

PURPOSES OF WRITING

When writing is your only alternative, you need to approach it with a pretty firm grip on its purposes. To try to talk about all the many purposes of writing would be almost futile. They vary not only from situation to situation, but also within situations themselves. Sifting grandly through all that, though, we come down to only two possible broad purposes for writing. They were recognized by the great thinkers of the ancient world, classical antiquity, Middle Ages, Renaissance, and Enlightenment. For all of them, and for us today, writing exists to these ends:

1. To delight
2. To teach

Traditionally, the emphasis has been on the second purpose. But the thing that all those earlier thinkers and writers recognized is that teaching occurs only after delight. That's a necessary reality of human nature. A writer can achieve delight in a couple of easy ways: by making us happy or by not making us angry.

In the military context, most of the delight that occurs will tend to be of the second sort. Military writers "delight" their readers by not making them angry. They avoid making them angry by ensuring that the substance, organization, style, and correctness of what they write allow it to be understood in one fast reading. Once the natural barriers to teaching have been broken down by delight, learning can take place.

Those natural barriers, by the way, are not unique to military readers. The thinkers who came up with the idea that effective writing must, by definition, be delightful teaching did so with a much larger and far more varied audience in mind: the human race. Part of the human condition, the very stuff that makes us what we are, is our ability to be distracted.

That's really a polite way of saying that people aren't as fond of liver as they are of apple pie. Given the right conditions—in this case, severe hunger and the guarantee of pie afterward—most folks will choke the liver down. So, too, with learning. Keep in mind that hunger is an essential ingredient. Without it, all the pie in the world won't entice you to eat the liver. Given that need, though, you will eat what's good for you. But the liver and the pie have to be a package deal; otherwise, the liver will get thrown out.

That's true of writing as well. It's not enough to have nothing more than delightful teaching. People can worry about that sort of self-improvement after duty hours. You also must have the *need* for it, and that need must be as strong as the severe hunger that causes people to eat the liver. You don't put out that kind of food if you don't have the catalyst of severe hunger. Likewise, you don't put out writing if you don't have a genuine need for it. If that sounds familiar, it's only because it's the fourth time I've made the point.

Before leaving this subject, we need to consider the matter of what gets taught. In a word, all kinds of things. Actually, however many things you have to talk about, you're going to talk about them toward one of two ends:

1. To inform
2. To persuade

It doesn't require much shrewdness to realize that many times (maybe most times) you must do both at the same time. For instance, suppose you want Airman Foster to pay for a wrench and a box of sockets. Before you can get a judgment against this person, you first need to demonstrate that Foster lost the property through negligence or willfully disposed of it. Whatever the case, information must precede persuasion.

Fight the urge to give more information than you need to give. Of course, papers that do nothing but inform have their place as well. Such writing is fundamentally historical; it gives us just the facts. But when that's all we need, that's all we want. It's a simple matter of economy.

Teaching, for the military writer, comes down to information and persuasion. Before you write your first word, make sure you know which of those two things you are trying to do. Armed with that crucial bit of knowledge, you can concentrate on ways to make what you write achieve your purpose.

The fundamental way to do that is through delight, to return to the earlier point. By design, I have emphasized a kind of negative delight—delight as the converse of anger. That's not the way to spend your entire career as a military writer. People in general, and military people in particular, like to do things in positive ways. With enough practice, you can approach delight positively. And that's what it will take: *practice*. Still, if you aren't all that sure of yourself at first, concentrate on writing things so that your reader won't be annoyed by the work you've done. Admittedly, that isn't a perfect solution, but then, this isn't a perfect world. And it will work most of the time.

WRITING AS THE LAST RESORT

At the beginning of this chapter we looked at the three means by which people generally communicate. You no doubt noticed that the one element all three have in common is words. You also must have noticed that the more we rely on words as a vehicle for understanding, the less effective our communications become. Beyond all the other reasons I have expressed or implied for using writing as the last resort, we need to take a moment or two to look at words.

Particularly, I want to look at why words don't seem to serve us as well as we might expect. Many explanations could be offered, but two seem especially important. The first has to do with what we know and how we think. Generally, the more experience we have with a given issue, the more ways we seem to look at it. Consequently, we may make something that is quite simple into something quite complex. By the same token, we may oversimplify things whose essence turns out to be very complicated.

A good illustration of that process is the way many people perform on multiple-choice tests. Those who know very little, unless luck is really guiding their pens, do poorly; those who know a whole lot about the material get passing marks, but not very high ones; those who know something about it tend to get the best grades. Why? The ignoramus simply guesses and lets the numbers fall where they will; the expert reads closely, so closely, in fact, that he reads between the lines to the extent that almost any answer could be correct. The student who has routinely prepared stands the best chance of doing well. Knowing more than the ignoramus and less than the expert, he has none of the encumbrances of either, and hence hits the target most of the time.

None of that is to argue against knowing a subject well. Far from it. Rather, my point is merely that what we do know (and how we use what we know when we think) will certainly influence the way we react to and understand words. Here's something that will show what I mean. Several words are printed below along with four possible definitions for each. Which do you think is correct?

1. Parameter
   a. boundary
   b. border
   c. constant
   d. perimeter
2. Infer
   a. imply
   b. conclude
   c. induce
   d. intuit
3. Billet
   a. position
   b. letter
   c. facility
   d. assignment
4. Disinterested
   a. bored
   b. uninterested
   c. unconnected
   d. objective
5. Caveat
   a. fish
   b. warning
   c. danger
   d. risk

In order, the correct choices are c, b, a, d, and b. If you got them all right, good for you; if you didn't, welcome to the human race. If you agreed with the dictionary definition maybe only two or three times, does that mean that you're stupid? It could. More than likely, though, it means that you colored the process of defining those five words with what you know, your past experiences, and perhaps even an assumed context for their use.

Incidentally, don't make the mistake of thinking that if you had been asked to define those words in a certain context, you would have done a whole lot better. If anything, your score might have been worse. Here's why.

Medieval thinkers were rather fond of making lists and creating categories. St. Augustine, the fifth-century bishop of Hippo, spent a good deal of his life thinking and writing about how people read. Based on a lot of different evidence gathered from other thinkers and his own experiences, he argued that it is possible to read the same passage in at least four different ways: literally, figuratively, morally, and anagogically (another way of saying mystically). He also says that each level of reading will open up new vistas of truth and understanding for the reader. Which level a reader can read on is a function of knowledge, experience, and brain power.

Outside certain theological and scholarly circles, we no longer actively attempt to gain our insights through multilevel reading, but that doesn't alter the fact that we have the capability to do so.

In fact, we sometimes do read on different levels simply because words, by their very nature, give us no choice. That's because many of them tend to have both denotative and connotative value. For example, the verb "to pinch" denotes squeezing between two hard surfaces. That same verb also connotes or implies a sneaky sort of theft. When you report that someone "pinched" your wallet, be sure the person taking the report understands a crime has occurred—if, indeed, one has. What one person might take as a figure of speech, another might take quite literally. When that happens, communications break down.

Words by themselves, or in context, will do as much to hamper understanding as they do to advance it as long as the people using them do not have the same knowledge, background, and brain power. The chances that we will write for someone who has those things in common with us are not good. Because of that, we need to take particular care to observe what the sixteenth-century English critic George Puttenham called decorum. "In all things [you write] . . . , use decency," he said. His message is simply this: *To communicate effectively, writers must take special pains to match the words they use with the context and audience for which they use them.*

No doubt about it, words can cause you some problems when you get ready to write. But the news is not all bad. Probably more than their counterparts in other professions, military writers can expect to share a number of significant things—vocabulary, contextual reference points, experience, and the like—with their readers.

On a communications playing field leveled by that kind of commonality, you might be able to do better than the 40 percent rate of understanding we know most writers achieve. Still, you probably won't do too much better. And that's because in human beings certain severe limitations and extraordinary capabilities exist almost side by side. That's another thing that gets in the way of our using words effectively. Take a minute to examine the table below, which measures a variety of functions in words per minute:

SPEED OF MENTAL FUNCTIONS
(words per minute)

Recognition	5,000–10,000
Thinking	1,000–2,000
Reading	200–300
Listening	120–160
Heavy reading	100–200
Writing	30–50
Note taking	15–25
Composing	0–?

Before we go any further, I should say that there are bound to be exceptions for each of the figures listed above. Someone who has taken a high-powered course in speed reading may be able to absorb the entire contents of a novel merely by placing his hand on the cover for a second or two. A person who cannot think without moving his lips to form each of the words will necessarily come in considerably under 1,000 words per minute. Lots of studies and even more practical experience have gone into coming up with the figures I have used. Whether there are occasional exceptions to them doesn't matter; what does matter is that they illustrate the relative abilities of most people well enough.

The implications of all that for writing ought to be pretty clear. Let's look at reading speed. Most of us get through a newspaper or a novel at 200 to 300 words a minute. That's light reading. Heavy reading—Chaucer, Dante, Shakespeare, or, say, the contents of your inbox—cuts reading speed about in half. At the same time, recognition—the very rapid processing of information—can proceed at a blinding rate. Obviously we don't recognize in words per se; but when we express the bioelectrical impulses of recognition in terms of words, the rate is 5,000 to 10,000 words per minute. We can *think* in words, though, and if somewhat slower than recognition, thinking still cracks right along.

Question: What's the mind supposed to do with its capacity to think at 1,000 to 2,000 words a minute while the eyes go through the morning's distribution at a tenth of that speed? Answer: Wander all over the place and introduce material that gets in the way of understanding any writing that isn't put together more or less flawlessly. The mind will do the same thing to you when you're listening to the 140 or so words per minute that your ears can take in. Unless those words are arranged in such a way as to let the mind record, understand, and mull them over almost at the same time, it will take its great capabilities and seek its amusement elsewhere.

Of course, during listening you get back some or all the things—feedback, body language, and so on—you lose with a written text. I have already noted their worth in helping us understand what's being said. They have a certain entertainment value, a capacity to delight, that writing has to produce in other ways. Indeed, it produces delight with the only tool available to the writer: words.

With that observation, we seem to have come full circle. Writing is the least efficient, least effective means of communication. Keep that in mind when you're tempted to put something on paper when a phone call or, better still, a walk down the street will do the job. Think of writing as the reserve force you commit only after everything has collapsed. *Think of writing as the last resort.*

4

Substance

Substance is the elusive stuff of writing. Because it is so elusive, many writers have a hard time trying to get hold of it. How many times have you said or heard someone else say, "I know what I want to write, but I'm having a little trouble finding the right words"? In most cases, that's just another way of saying, "I don't know what I'm talking about." When that happens, a deficiency in substance is often the problem.

By substance I mean a solid knowledge of the material at issue. There's more. That knowledge must be available in ways that show sound reasoning. Further, such reasoning should reflect the writer's clear purpose, careful thought, good perceptions, and a spark or two of imagination. Substance is the bedrock of any writing you may be asked to do. Without it, the best you can hope to do is put together a series of empty phrases that may, if you're lucky, seem to have some utility.

A writer who has mastered the conventions of grammar and English usage may turn out things that, at first glance, look pretty good. So may the writer who knows something about style. But however correct or polished, the absence of genuine substance makes such writing only so useful. An equally serious flaw is the burial of short but substantial material under a mountain of words simply to give what you've written the look of substance.

Before going on to address the specific issues this chapter takes up, I cannot resist making one critical point about substance: *If you haven't got anything to say, don't say it.* And even more important in the context of this book, don't write it.

HAVING SOMETHING TO SAY

Most of the time when you get asked to write, there *will* be something to say. And most of the time you're going to know what that something is. That being the case, the question you need to wrestle with is not so much *what* to say but rather *how much.*

Consider this trivial analogy: If water is the substance and your purpose is to shower, how might you use it to your best advantage? First of all, you would focus the showerhead and shower curtain so that water will stay within the shower enclosure. Next, you would turn the water on when you were more or less ready to bathe, not ten minutes before. Finally, you would adjust the temperature. Though it won't hurt you, a cold shower isn't too pleasant, and a hot shower will scald you. Odds are that you would opt for a warm shower.

So, too, with your writing. To begin with, you have to stay within the enclosure. That is, you need to fit what you write to the format prescribed to you. If you get outside it, you make a mess and defeat your purpose. Second, don't waste any of your assets with false starts. Finally, avoid extremes that can, at best, make you uncomfortable and, at worst, be harmful to you and your reader.

The principle at work here has, as you might expect, a debt to antiquity. Though he didn't come up with the idea, Aristotle expressed it best. Most of his philosophical precepts are contained in his notion of the golden mean— the middle ground between two extremes. Getting to that middle ground, however, puts a little pressure on the judgment of those who try to approach it. For instance, the golden mean between cowardice and foolhardiness is courage. The marine who runs from his foxhole to bash in the head of an enemy soldier with a rock is foolhardy. He could have eliminated his opponent without leaving the relative safety of his own position. All he needed to do was call in an air strike or artillery fire. But in the absence of airpower or an artillery battery or even a rifle, that marine's act suddenly becomes courageous, so courageous, in fact, that it will likely be recognized with some kind of medal.

Likewise, in the matter of substance, writers must use their best judgment to ensure that what they write does two things:

1. Offers information of just enough quality and in just enough quantity to do what it sets out to do
2. Takes into account the context in which and for which it is being produced

GETTING MORE INFORMATION

Everything I have said up to now supposes that you will know what you're talking about when you sit down to write. But what if you don't? Or worse yet, what if you're not sure? Let's deal with that last possibility first. Here's the acid test: If you haven't got a specific, concrete example to illustrate every point you want to make, then (for our purposes here) you don't know what you're talking about. And neither will your reader.

What should a reader make of an information paper that reads like the following?

> The leadership course our noncommissioned officers attended last month is paying big dividends. Our training officer is making plans for even more of them to attend the next session. The absence of those attending the course will hurt the unit, but the sacrifice will be worth it.

Or how might a promotion board respond to a fitness report with the following narrative?

> Major Munson continues to prove he is a first-class officer. He does things better than his contemporaries do. His office is extremely efficient and, thus, able to turn out a great deal of work in a short time. This officer performs well under pressure, and he is able to motivate his subordinates to do the same.

Looking at these examples, you should notice that the mechanics of both are generally correct; both can be understood in a single, fast reading. However, neither is a satisfactory piece of writing because neither really says anything. Both make some fairly bold claims, but why should we accept them? Is there any evidence to give us the slightest reason to believe they are true? Where are the specific, concrete examples that show us that Major Munson "does things better than his contemporaries" or that "the leadership course our noncommissioned officers attended last month is paying big dividends"? Perhaps such examples exist in the heads of the people who wrote those passages. But what good does that do their readers?

Sometimes a particular format will give you less room to work in than you would like. Writers in the military just have to come to terms with that sort of inconvenience. And it is possible. To return to the shower analogy: When you go to the field, do you stop bathing? Of course not. Instead, you might use a bucket shower that will hold four quarts of sun-heated water. By planning carefully and by paying attention to what you're doing, you'll get yourself clean and still have plenty of water for your final rinse.

In many cases, getting more information isn't doing more digging. Rather, it's a matter of sifting through what you've already dug up and using it to your and your reader's best advantage. If space is limited, don't try to talk in cosmic terms. Select your most important material and develop it fully. On the other hand, if you have room, you may expand your work, as long as you don't overdo it. It's a matter of judgment.

Take a few seconds to scan this revision of an earlier example:

> The leadership course our noncommissioned officers attended last month is paying big dividends. In the three weeks since Sergeants Wilbur, Bonney, and Jordan returned, they have spent more than sixty hours conducting counseling sessions for thirty-seven airmen. Of that group, six have radically altered their patterns of behavior. Two who were chronic complainers have not made a negative remark in nearly two weeks. Three others who were habitual no-shows for physical training have not missed a formation in eight consecutive sessions. The sixth individual, typically a loner, seems to be entering more into the ongoing life of the organization. Two days ago he requested to be placed on the Morale Committee, and I have hope that he will continue to try to become more involved. Specifically, the way he seems to be committing himself to the planning for new game room equipment has me particularly encouraged. Anyway, he appears to be benefiting from the kinds of things Sergeants Wilbur, Bonney, and Jordan are doing since their return to the unit.
>
> Our training officer is making plans for even more . . .

There's an instance of too much information. Midway through the revised example, the reader is ready to scream: "All right! I believe you! Let's get this thing over with." Too much can be as bad as too little. Both gluttony and starvation make the stomach hurt and injure the body. The object is moderation. Use your judgment wisely.

On judgment, one final word: When you're in the business of getting more information, remember that you're getting it for the reader. Get enough to guarantee his understanding, and set the rest aside. If you can do that without having to ask anyone or without having to do extra research, then you do know what you're talking about.

On this basis, should it turn out that you don't know the subject well enough to give your writing the substance it needs, you can save yourself a lot of time by giving up any notion you had of writing the first word until you really have the stuff you need to begin writing. How do you get that?

The same way you get anything else you need: by talking to people and doing research.

KNOWING THE SUBJECT

Some two centuries ago Alexander Pope, the brilliant and short-fused English poet, warned, "A little learning is a dang'rous thing." Potentially, as chapter 3 already suggested, knowing too much has its dangers too. The more you know, the fewer absolutes there are to fall back on. When absolutes dissolve, so do easy answers. Beyond that built-in hazard of knowledge, there is the risk of becoming too fond of what you know.

Certainly that seemed to be what happened to the writer of our last example. The more he explored detail, the more intrigued with it he became. In very little space, substance had overridden purpose. If his intent had been to inform his reader that such and such program was succeeding, he took no time at all to get himself—and us—off track. Once that happened, the effectiveness of his communication took a nosedive.

Pope doesn't explicitly warn us about the risks of knowing too much because that really isn't a problem for most of us. Our problem has usually been trying to show how much we know. Whether we write that way by design, the result is no less disruptive to the communications process. Pope does, however, speak indirectly to that point as an editor of Shakespeare: "Brevity is the soul of wit."

5

Organization

"Before you try to write this paper, you need to have an outline." I don't remember which of my teachers said that to me the first time. It doesn't really matter, though, because all did at one time or another. By the time I got to the sixth grade, I automatically began any writing assignment with an outline. Sometimes I would really go all out and create very elaborate sentence outlines; other times, I would go about it less grandly. But either way, I would come up with something like the following:

I. Introduction
    A. Background and opening sentences
    B. Major points for discussion
II. Body
    A. Development of first point
        1. Example of point
        2. Discussion
    B. Development of second point
        1. Example of point
        2. Discussion
    C. Development of nth point
        1. Example of point
        2. Discussion
III. Conclusion
    A. Summary
    B. Concluding statement

Does that look great or what? It's beautifully organized. It addresses the three points every piece of writing must have: a beginning, middle, and end.

It looks neat. Complete. The trouble is, I couldn't work with it, and I still can't. But I couldn't let go easily. When I first learned about outlines, I was extremely taken by the order they represented. They were so . . . well, organized.

What I didn't realize for many years is that the very order they represent is the thing that makes them so hard to use. And I had been taught the wrong thing about outlines, too. All my teachers had said that an outline would help me organize my writing. That isn't quite the way they work. An outline helps writers see if the logical relationships in their writing are good. If they are, the writing, by definition, is organized; if they aren't, the outline isn't going to help.

The second thing I didn't realize was that the stuff I put after Roman numerals I and III was utterly worthless. All that mattered to me was that every bit of it was somehow part of a very precise format I wasn't supposed to alter. Never mind that all that stuff distracted me from getting to the meat of the outline; that is, everything after Roman numeral II. Worse, it led me to believe that I had already said something when, in fact, I had merely been running in place.

The other problem I couldn't come to terms with was that my ideas would not always fit neatly into the rigid outline form. You know the rules: If you have a capital A, then you must have a capital B; if you have an Arabic 1, then you must have an Arabic 2. Well, I didn't always have a capital B or an Arabic 2. I solved such problems by cramming the unbalanced capital A or Arabic 1 into other parts of the outline where they could sort of fit without disrupting too much.

By putting something where it really didn't fit, I weakened the outline's organization and thereby defeated its purpose. I knew it, too, but that didn't always stop me. That's because I believed I had only one other alternative: to throw away the idea that didn't fit the format. As I became a little more sophisticated, though, I discovered a third alternative: to keep the material where I had wanted it to be in the first place and then balance it with a bit of padding. That way, I reckoned to make everyone happy. In practice, of course, that solution didn't work very well. It preserved the outline's format, but it presented me with many new problems. One of the most serious was how to turn that padding into something that didn't look like padding. Usually I couldn't, and that invariably annoyed whomever my reader happened to be.

Ironic and stupid as it seems, outlines and the rigid format that governs the way we are supposed to use them defeated nearly everything I wrote while I was in school. Then one day, in a moment of surprising insight, it occurred to me that I had allowed something that should have been serving me to become my master instead. For most of my life I had been throwing away good boards, or sawing them in half, because I didn't have the right kind of tools to use them properly. Once I realized that, I stopped using outlines as a way to get organized.

Walking away from them is hard at first. After all, most of your life you've been told to use them. And when you used them in conjunction with really having something to say, chances are that what you wrote turned out more or less all right. That is to say, you probably got by without having to do a major rewrite. Chances are, too, that what you wrote could have been much better if ordered in a slightly different way.

Consider the way outlines look. They have precise places for everything, and everything must fit into those places. Outlines have a sequential order we cannot escape. And whether it should, that sequence implies priorities. Such linear ordering appeals to most people because it approximates the way we think.

Students of the human brain have made some remarkable discoveries about how it works. To oversimplify years of research and study, the brain's left side works in linear fashion: It is logical and systematic. We solve problems with the left side of the brain. In contrast, the right side functions randomly. Creative, inventive, and undisciplined, it functions in altogether different ways.

More than two thousand years before those findings came to light, Plato concluded that the brain had two distinct parts, a reasonable half and a passionate half. To him, a person was like a chariot driver being pulled along by two strong horses. Harnessed together, the horses would keep to the road, but if the driver slacked the reins in favor of either, the chariot would wind up in a ditch.

The notion of the brain's equal parts lasted through the Middle Ages and Renaissance. Abandoning the metaphor of the two horses, philosophers and writers wrestling with how the mind works began to explain certain kinds of behavior in terms of gender. Reason, for example, represented the male half of the brain; the female half was unreasonable or passionate. When the passionate half of the brain dominated, disastrous consequences were inevitable. Those thinkers (mostly men) were quick to point to what happened in the Garden of Eden as evidence. Early in the twentieth century, psychologist Carl Jung accounted for the consequences of this male-female struggle by coining the terms "introvert" and "extrovert."

The thing connecting all those theories with scientific fact is the dual nature of the brain: The brain not only consists of two parts, but those parts perform distinctly different functions as well. Traditionally, the two parts have been regarded as equal. The fact is, they aren't.

The left side of the brain, that reasonable, linear half that solves problems, represents some 15 percent of the brain's capacity; the balance belongs to the right side. For all that, the left side seems to control the right side most of the time. That news might please a medieval scholar, but the military writer can't take much pleasure in it. Innovation, creativity, and imagination all belong to the right side of the brain. The question is, How can we get to them?

Of one thing we can be sure: Outlining is not the way.

BRAINSTORMING

Given the thousands of years our culture has socialized us away from the right half of the brain, it's no great wonder that we resist using it. Indeed, if you think about it in a similar light, the outline is just another case of such socialization. Outlining inhibits your access to the right side of the brain. Brainstorming does not.

By brainstorming I mean giving your mind the chance to have outrageous, random, unrealistic, inventive, foolish, exciting, improbable, imaginative, and undisciplined thoughts. Thoughts of that sort are the fabric of daydreams and free association. Turning them to your advantage, though, is easier than you might suppose.

First of all, you need to get rid of anything that might encourage a takeover by the left brain. That means eliminating linear schemes. In other words, the last thing you want to do is make a list. Why? Because even without numbers running down the left margin, a list implies priorities. Given an unnumbered list of household chores, most people will start at the top and work down. That's the way we are. That's also the left side of the brain in action.

In lieu of a list, try using something that looks like Figure 4.

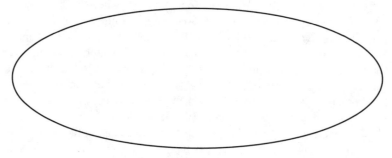

Figure 4.

By design, I have avoided the precise regularity of a circle. The military relies too much on circles for you to be oblivious to the order the circular shape implies. For that matter, if you own a conventional watch or clock, you're unlikely to move around a circle in any fashion but clockwise, no matter where you start on it. The oblong shape I've suggested may not overcome your every impulse toward an orderly progression around it. Then again, it might.

You have endured a lot to get to this point, but now that we're here, we can move pretty quickly. To help us do that, I want to work with an extended fictional example that puts you on the hot seat. Suppose that your boss has asked you for a paper on reenlistment, and suppose the paper has to be on her desk in two hours, sooner if you can manage it. Assume that you have to get moving on this project with no more information than you have right now.

Draw an oblong shape that looks like Figure 5 in the middle of a blank piece of paper or on a chalkboard.

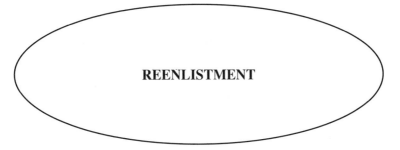

Figure 5.

As if you needed any more pressure, ask someone (or do it yourself) to time you for a minute and a half or two minutes. When the timing starts, randomly draw radial lines from your oblong, labeling each with a word or symbol representing the thought that caused you to draw the line in the first place. As you draw lines, avoid going in the same direction more than a couple of times in a row. That is, if you start at the lower right of the oblong, move to the top to begin your second line, over to the far left for the third, and so on.

Here's the key: Focus your concentration on the topic as fully as you can. Remember, you don't have any real format constraints. If drawing lines doesn't suit you, don't draw lines. The object of this technique is to help you get your ideas out where you can use them. However you go about it, a minute or so after you begin you should have something that looks like Figure 6.

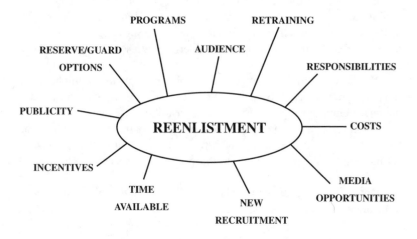

Figure 6.

That's a fair amount of material for a little more than a minute's thought. Before we try to make sense of it, let's look at why we go about getting it this way. If you think back to the words-per-minute diagram in chapter 3, you'll recall a substantial difference in writing speed and thinking speed. The hand can't catch up with the mind, and the mind's too active to wait around for long. It's going to do other things, and if the hand isn't ready, the idea dies where it falls. By jotting down only a word, phrase, or symbol, the hand can increase its efficiency considerably and do a better job of keeping up with the brain. Clearly some things will still slip through the cracks, but a lot will get saved.

Now you can't leave those words and phrases for too long because you'll forget what they really mean. Soon after you do your brainstorming, you will need to make some notes on each word, phrase, or symbol to remind yourself what it meant. Keep this process as painless as you can. Write no more than you need for remembering what you meant. For the sake of legibility, it's best to do that on a separate piece of paper. What you write should be no more detailed than the following:

> Incentives: reenlistment bonuses, special assignments, etc., for person reenlisting. For person or unit getting reenlistment?

Publicity: both before and after the fact. What exists? Needs?

Programs: What exists? Needs?

Media opportunities: Can we use media in new, better, cheaper ways?

Retraining: Opportunities for new skills?

Audience: Who are we trying to sell to?

New recruitment: Cheaper than reenlistment? Young vets? Ex-service civilians?

Costs: Do we have the $? How much more needed? Ideas for spending excess $?

Reserve/guard options: Reenlist to get out of active service early? To come on active duty from reserve/guard?

Time available: How much do we have? Suspense dates? Schedule development?

Responsibilities: Who's in charge at what level? Responsibilities of recruiter?

Though you won't use this "translation" as anything but a reference, it's nevertheless a good idea not to put things down in any sort of order. This sample translation imposes a kind of artificial randomness that will help keep a simple reference sheet from becoming a linear grouping of priorities.

GROUPINGS AND NATURAL HEADINGS
Ultimately, groupings do become an issue, but it's only at this point that you need to worry about them. Here's how to go about it. Get several different colors of writing instruments that you can use on the same surface on which you did your brainstorming. Consulting your reference sheet as necessary, group related ideas together. This process sounds a bit strange, but it's easy enough to run through (see Figure 7).

In attempting to group your ideas together, you will be pleased to find that they do not represent intellectual anarchy after all, but the workings of a capable and generally ordered mind turning out potentially related and

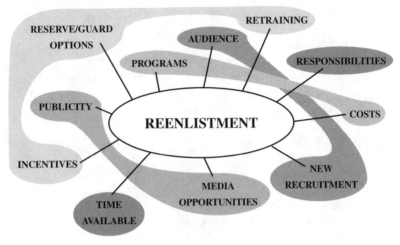

Figure 7.

probably usable thoughts in a random fashion. Allowing the process to play itself out in this way, we take maximum advantage of both our head and hand.

Obviously, we cannot continue to work with several colored blobs. The next step is to assign those blobs names—to give them *headings*. For the examples at hand, the headings in Figure 8 seem as good as any.

AUDIENCE

RESPONSIBILITIES

PROGRAMS

TIME

PUBLICITY

INCENTIVES

Figure 8.

Once more, and by intention, we want to stay away from a linear presentation of the headings because we still want to avoid giving them relative weight. Given what we know at this point, how could we rank them anyway? Think back to the original instructions you received: Write a paper on reenlistment. Before you can do a whole lot more, you need to go back to your boss and get some guidance. By the way, you have time to do that. Everything that's happened up to now has taken, at most, fifteen minutes.

Suppose you take the six headings and head for the boss's office. When you get there, all you need to say is, "I have six issues I can address. What direction do you want this paper to take?" Right there is when you're going to get your purpose. You'll know for sure, for instance, whether you are writing to inform or to persuade. And with any luck, you'll also know that some of the stuff, which might be useful in one kind of paper, won't fit. That means you can dump it, and dump it without hesitation.

That brings us to another major advantage of using brainstorming as a means of organizing your work. Apart from saving the time it would have taken you to write out everything represented by each of those headings, you'll avoid attachment to particular passages that seem too good to drop. If a couple of headings have to fall out, so what? It will save you from writing that one magnificent paragraph that it would be a crime to get rid of.

Let's say that the second meeting with the boss results in this comment: "Time isn't really an issue right now, so don't worry about it in your paper. And we've already fixed responsibility for reenlistment. That means there's no need to mention it either. We probably ought to say something about everything else on your list, though. What we want to do is let General Erskine know what our programs are and who we're pitching to."

With guidance like that, pulling your paper together in the time remaining should be fairly easy. But without those six headings you took in to the boss, you never would have received that sort of guidance. Of course you wouldn't have had the headings so quickly, if at all, had you not gone through the process of brainstorming. What makes this approach particularly sound in terms of logical relationships is that *your thoughts and ideas produce your headings.*

Often—too often—writers try to reverse that process. Just because you have a heading doesn't mean that you're going to have anything to put under it. By starting with what goes below the heading, you are able to group things naturally. What that really means is that in the finished paper things will be where they're supposed to be; it means your writing will have a natural organization that will permit very rapid reading.

To be sure, there are many other techniques that will help you get started and aid you with your organization, but none is quicker or simpler than the kind of brainstorming we have been looking at here. If you remain unconvinced of the value of this process, let me suggest one more dimension to it. By way of doing that, I need to digress for a brief look at the nineteenth-century German philosopher Georg Wilhelm Friedrich Hegel.

Hegel did a lot to promote the dialectic, a system for getting things done. This system is summed up in Figure 9.

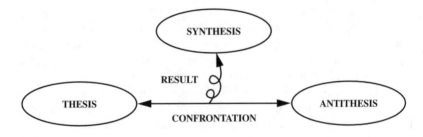

Figure 9.

That is, if we confront one idea (thesis) with its opposite (antithesis), the result will be a kind of compromise (synthesis). He goes on to say that the synthesis, by definition, is a new thesis. It's only a matter of time before it is confronted with a new antithesis. Hegel argues that if these confrontations were to continue long enough, the final synthesis would, in fact, be nothing less than truth.

Now before deciding to ignore Hegel's dialectic, consider the real-world example in Figure 10.

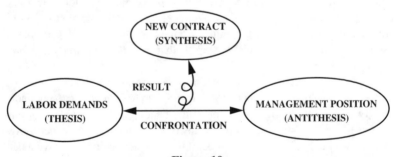

Figure 10.

Apply this illustration to the automobile industry. To see the continuing nature of the dialectic, you need only consider that the contract the workers signed to end the strike in year X will make them go back on strike in year Y.

And the contract they happily sign to end the new strike will have them back out on the picket line come year Z. We can only hope (along with Hegel) that each new contract brings labor and management a little closer to truth.

Brainstorming, as we have looked at it in this chapter, will not necessarily lead you to truth; it will, however, allow you to engage in a kind of successive reasoning that works a lot like Hegel's dialectic. To see how, let's return to the original assignment: Write a paper on reenlistment. You will recall it took little more than a minute to come up with eleven ideas on the topic. You did that without any guidance and against a deadline of two hours. Because this process moves quickly, you could also do the following suggestion in those two hours. And you could do it without additional guidance, though that's not the best way to go at this stage, if you have any choice.

In this example, you do have a choice. You know what the boss wants, or rather, what she doesn't want. The fastest and simplest way to be sure you have enough to give her is to fine-tune the information you already have. Go back to the four headings you were told to treat, and at this time, look at what each is made up of:

Audience	*Programs*
Audience	Programs
New recruitment	Costs

Publicity	*Incentives*
Publicity	Incentives
Media opportunities	Reserve/guard options
	Retraining

If you are puzzled because the headings are repeated in the lists below them, refer to the reference sheet. Remember, too, that in selecting heading titles, we want to pick words that naturally and broadly account for all the ideas in a group. Some repetition is likely; in this particular case, it's inevitable.

Let's look at publicity; within that group, let's focus on media opportunities. Suppose that when you jotted down that phrase you didn't know precisely what its implications might be. Maybe you thought that there might be some unexploited media opportunities that could be of use in a reenlistment campaign. Before you start to write about them, though, it makes sense to give them a bit more thought. A good way to do that is by going back to where the idea came from in the first place. In about a minute's time, you can discover that by media opportunities you meant something like Figure 11.

Figure 11.

Of course you need to make your reference sheet quickly, and then do a fast job of grouping thoughts and ideas. As you do that, if you discover that something, for example, use of military as "experts" on news shows or military sports, needs a closer look, it will be easy enough to brainstorm it. Just one more minute will give you Figure 12.

Figure 12.

Whether any or all of this material finds its way into your paper—which you still have better than an hour and a half to produce—is a matter of judgment. That you have it available, though, certainly puts you on solid footing as you get ready to start writing.

CONVERSION TO OUTLINES

A couple of pages ago I noted that the groups of ideas coming out of brainstorming were the things that generated the headings. Likewise, the headings (and everything under them) generate the conclusion of the paper. You'll see how neatly all that fits together as you go through the last of your prewriting activities.

Once you have sufficient material to write about—that is, substance—you can finally put your headings in some sort of linear order. Before doing that, let's come to terms with this emphatic point: *It frequently takes a lot of work after you have brainstormed a subject to come up with something to say about it.* What? This all seemed too easy. There had to be a catch.

Look, brainstorming won't do a thing for you in the area of substance unless you happen to know something about the ideas that the process generates. What it does give you are the ideas themselves. It's up to you to get any additional information you need to bring them to life. Don't let any of that dissuade you from using this valuable organizational tool. If it can organize your thoughts (and you've already seen that it can), it can also organize your research efforts. With that kind of a head start, you haven't got much to gripe about.

For the sake of this extended example, let's assume that you have all the substance you need to make this paper succeed. On that basis, let's go back to our aim or purpose. According to the boss, "What we want to do is let General Erskine know what our programs are and who we're pitching to." That means the purpose of this paper is to inform. Knowing that, you might arrange the material along these lines:

Programs

Audience

Incentives

Publicity

That's about as close to an outline as you need to come. If time weren't an issue (you have used up about forty minutes of the two hours), you might want to go ahead and include the different ideas each heading represents. In any case, you have more than enough to produce a well-organized paper without further delay.

FINDING THE BOTTOM LINE

There are plenty of good reasons for doing all you can to organize your writing well. The most important, in a military context, is to ensure that anything you write can be understood in one fast reading. Headings are a major part of your insurance. If they are instrumental in the writing of a good paper (and they are), they should be no less instrumental in the understanding of it. Why deprive the reader of the very things that make your job so much easier than it would be without them? You shouldn't. Instead, let headings function as signposts to get the reader through your writing directly, quickly, and without confusion.

The other thing that will help your reader is for you to put the bottom line or conclusion at the *top* of the paper. How many times have you flipped quickly through a document in search of its conclusion? How many times have you seen your supervisor go straight to the last page of a paper to find and act on its bottom line? More than once is the likely answer to both questions.

Of course you can't put your bottom line at the top of the page if you aren't sure what it is yourself. That's something else you must know before you write. Finding it really isn't that hard, especially if the aim of your writing is information. To discover the bottom line in informational writing, you need only summarize the essence of your material and state it in the form of a brisk sentence or two. The bottom line of our example looks like this: We have X reenlistment programs. Our target audience is Y.

In a paper whose purpose is persuasion, the bottom line or conclusion is a statement of whatever you want your reader to do. In persuasive writing, the relationship of groups of ideas, headings, and conclusion must be direct and obvious. Let's go back to the reenlistment example to see how those things fit together. Suppose, after seeing your six headings, your boss said, "General Erskine has a solid grip on our programs and target audience. But he's not happy with the kind of response we've been getting. My guess is that he's going to want some new ideas on incentives. Run what you have on incentives around the staff, and give me a paper as quickly as you can."

Before you do any writing in this case, the first thing you should do is brainstorm incentives. Having the focus the boss has given you, you ought to be able to develop groups and headings very quickly. Taking that material around the staff will no doubt cause you to make some changes. Incorporate as many as you need to, get rid of any excess, and set up your headings in the linear pattern that best supports the conclusion generated by your brainstorming and staff coordination.

That conclusion may come out as a declarative statement:

> Reenlistment incentives appeal only to a first-term population.

Or it may be a recommendation:

> I recommend we allow second-termers to reenlist for training in a new specialty.

It might also be a combination of the two:

> Reenlistment incentives need more publicity. I recommend contracting the X corporation to develop a new campaign for general use before 1 November.

Incidentally, the first of those possible conclusions may sound more like the bottom line of an information paper. But if you knew that General Erskine believes that reenlistment incentives have general appeal, you would realize that getting him to accept your conclusion is going to take some heavy-duty persuasion.

That means that everything in the paper you are getting ready to write must be directed toward that end. And if you've done your homework, it will be. Here's why. Using this process honestly, you cannot keep an idea that doesn't have something specific and concrete behind it; and you cannot have a group without ideas to make it up. Nor can you have a heading without a group. Finally, you can't have a conclusion without headings. It's all a simple matter of cause and effect:

- Because you have specifics, you therefore have ideas.
- Because you have ideas, you therefore have groups.
- Because you have groups, you therefore have headings.
- Because you have headings, you therefore have a conclusion.

To translate that into schematic terms, see Figure 13.

This pattern of organization will help you write an orderly paper; it will help your reader follow your writing quickly and easily. Don't deprive him or her of it.

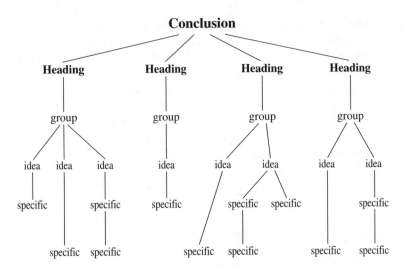

Figure 13.

Finding the bottom line is not hard. If your aim is to inform, then summarize the essence of what you have to say in a single sentence. On the other hand, if your aim is to persuade, follow specifics through groups and headings to their natural conclusion, which you also can express in a sentence. Either way, you have access to the heart of the paper before you begin to write it. Why not give the reader the same kind of access early on?

KILLING THE O. HENRY ENDING

O. Henry was the pen name taken by William Sydney Porter, a writer of short stories. He made the unexpected ending the trademark of his work, and it is on that kind of surprising turn of events that his reputation rests. You may remember reading one of his more famous stories, "The Gift of the Magi."

The plot has a newly married couple, very much in love and very much out of money, sitting around and listening to their stomachs growl. They try all sorts of things to get money, but with no luck. As Christmas approaches, it becomes clear that neither will have a present to give the other. The two pass the time trying to forget their misery—she by fooling with her very long and exquisite hair, he by looking at his heirloom pocket watch.

O. Henry strings us along for a few more pages before Christmas finally arrives. When it does, we see the young husband receiving a handsome watch fob for a pocket watch he no longer has. We learn that he has exchanged the watch for enough money to buy a set of fine combs for his wife. She, alas, is bald as an egg, having sold her hair to buy the watch fob.

If you like that sort of twist, and a lot of folks do, go to the library. That's what the people who read your writing can do as well. From O. Henry they want the O. Henry ending; from you they want the bottom line. And they want it where they can get to it: up front.

No doubt your various schoolteachers preached the virtues of keeping the reader in suspense. That's fine if you're writing to entertain, but not on the job. In the military there isn't time for suspense, even if there were a place for it. Busy readers know that. That's why they frantically leaf through the mounds of paper in their inboxes in search of bottom lines. Help them out by not hiding anything from them.

Here's the thing: When your boss asks you to write something, however good or poor the guidance, he is asking you to confirm or deny something that he likely has at least a tentative feeling about. In many cases, the feeling may be considerably stronger than that. By having easy access to your conclusion on the same topic, your reader can look at it right away and say: "That's what I thought, too." He can stop reading right there and go on to other things if he needs to. That's efficient.

If, on the other hand, the boss doesn't agree with the conclusion, its early appearance in the paper, and the use of headings throughout, will help him read quickly and without getting lost. The very quickness of that reading will do a lot to sway the reader over to your position. Persuading someone predisposed against your position is never easy. If your writing isn't orderly, economical, and devoted to supporting your bottom line, you haven't got a prayer.

Badly organized writing is evidence of a badly organized mind. No one's going to accept the conclusions of a badly organized mind. By the same token, orderly writing bespeaks an orderly mind. And an orderly mind, even if we disagree with it, demands our consideration. *When you write, you are presenting not only your ideas but also yourself.* Present both in the most attractive package you can. As should be very clear by now, good organization is a large part of that package. So is style, which leads to the next chapter.

6

Style

At any given time there are probably at least thirty writing books on the market with the word "style" in their titles. Each year some go out of print and an equal number come in to replace them, which shows, at the very least, two things: First, that writing style is something a lot of people are concerned about; and second, that much of what gets said about it is either repetitive or misunderstood.

That you're reading this book suggests that you have some interest in writing style. You have probably heard dozens of definitions of it. Maybe there are so many because people who write about style want to say something that will be true for all people for all time. I can't do that, and I'm not about to try. Within the finite context of military writing, though, I will offer this observation: *Good style is whatever it takes to make your writing communicate its substance quickly, clearly, and directly.*

Once you have a context, the audience, more than any other factor, must govern your style. In the military, you usually write for a military audience. Branch of service aside, the thing all members of this vast audience share is a distinct shortage of time. They are jealous of it and will do anything they can to protect it, including ignoring writing they know is going to take a long time to get through.

Quite simply, then, you must write well. And you must write for your audience. That means you cannot indulge yourself by trying to be literary, clever, or erudite. Decide on what you need to say, then say it. And be quick, clear, and direct about it. Any time you can save your reader will bring you a lot more renown than a long-winded tour de force of your best verbal flourishes.

ACTIVE VERSUS PASSIVE CONSTRUCTIONS

The most obvious way to save your readers time is to reduce the number of words you give them to read. One practical way to do that is to get rid of passive constructions. That may be easier said than done, though, because they remain common currency in military writing. Passive constructions are such a part of writing in the military that it may seem wrong not to use them. Well, it isn't.

Military writers are by no means the only culprits. Government writing in general is filled with the passive voice. In fact, here's an example of what could well be the model for the perfect government sentence:

> The mouse was eaten by the cat.

That sentence is seven words long. By getting rid of three of them, we can turn it into a model for the perfect military sentence:

> The mouse was eaten.

Never mind by what or whom. It may have been an act of God. Who knows?

In the passive voice the emphasis clearly is not on the doer. That, no doubt, is why military writers favor it. Here's what I mean: Which of these two sentences would you want your boss to read?

> The departure course was computed incorrectly.

> I computed the departure course incorrectly.

The prudent writer tends to emphasize the mistake rather than the person making it. But that's nonsense, really, and here's why. If the mistake is serious, do you honestly think the boss is going to let it pass without finding out who made it? Of course not. No one is going to let a sentence like this—"Two five-ton ammunition trucks have been wrecked on the road to Wildflecken"—pass without asking, Who was driving?

By the same token, if the mistake isn't serious (or if it isn't a mistake at all), you can't offer self-preservation as an argument for using the passive voice. There is no reason to write the following:

> Two of the missing rifles have been found.

Instead, you can write this:

> I found two of the missing rifles.

Not only is the second sentence shorter, but it also gives the reader more information than the first one.

Don't use the passive voice as a way of taking the heat off the doer. If the mouse was eaten by the cat, simply tell us:

> The cat ate the mouse.

It makes absolutely no difference to the mouse, but it makes a big difference to the person who has to read about the incident. First of all, the active voice supports the kind of organization we looked at in the last chapter: It puts the bottom line up front. That saves time. Second, it takes fewer words to say something in the active voice than it does in the passive voice—between 20 and 30 percent fewer, as a rule. Think about that for a second. If you were to take a typical military document that was ten pages long and strip out the passive voice, the revision would be seven or eight pages long. In terms of reading time, that's a substantial reduction.

Not all military writers use the passive voice to hide or protect the doer. Often they use it out of a sense of unworthiness: How can I, a mere ensign, presume to push a captain around? Face to face, the answer is you can't. On paper, though, if you're writing for the admiral, you certainly can. Chances are, in a face-to-face context the admiral would come to the point himself—and directly, too. Writing in his behalf, don't make him seem reluctant to say what needs to be said. If you have forgotten the section in chapter 1 that deals with writing for someone else, go back and reread it.

But regardless of whether the admiral is actually going to sign a paper on, say, painting bulkheads, if such a paper tells people what, when, why, where, or how to do things, it ought to tell them in the active voice. Don't worry a whole lot about whether you're worthy enough to come right out and say stuff. Assume that you are until someone tells you otherwise.

Some people write in the passive voice because their supervisors won't allow them to use personal pronouns. The first person "I" is at the top of many people's hit lists. Whether that's because of something they learned years ago in elementary school or a variation of the unworthiness theme (the supervisor decides that subordinate writers are not worthy to intrude themselves) doesn't matter. Folks who write in the passive voice aren't doing much to promote effective military writing.

Suppose, for instance, you have such a supervisor. Suppose, too, you must write a short paper asking permission to hire a temporary clerk for three months because one in the Finance Office is taking maternity leave. Part of your paper might read like this:

> This position will be vacated by Mrs. Martha C. Richards on 15 August. Bookkeeping support will be needed during her absence. Request a temporary clerk be approved.

How awful it is to read stuff like that. Its passive tone suggests a passive person who has been overtaken by events.

Recast in the active voice, the passage has quite a different tone:

> Mrs. Martha T. Richards vacates her position on 15 August. I need bookkeeping support during her maternity leave. Please approve a temporary clerk.

Even with the addition of the word "please," the revised version in the active voice does not whine at the reader the way the passive version does. It also happens to be four words shorter.

Using the first person "I" is fine if it gets the job done *and* if it isn't overworked. If you use it too much, you come off looking like an egomaniac; if you don't use it at all, you come off looking like a semiliterate by writing things such as: "Request a temporary secretary be approved." Good grief. And here—crisp, martial, and cryptic—is a typical response: Concur with this request.

Question: Does this mean the person signing the paper agrees? If her intention was to write a declarative sentence, she failed. As the next chapter explains, what we have here is a sentence fragment. In the imperative mood, of course, it is a sentence that says, [You will] concur with this request. But we know that isn't the intent of the response. All the writer wanted to say is, I agree. Or more simply, yes.

The point of the whole example is to show that outlawing personal pronouns generally, and "I" in particular, is a way to encourage bad writing. Yes, I know you live in the real world, but before you roll over altogether, take the time to talk to your supervisor on this point of style one more time. And don't do it at a time when you are almost certain to fail—in the middle of a crash program of some kind, for example. If, after that talk, the answer is still no, then fine. But don't do anything on your own to compound that error once you no longer have to.

Sometimes there are good stylistic reasons to use the passive voice, but I'm not going to draw your attention to such examples because I don't want to dilute the point I'm trying to make here: *Unless you have no choice, do not use the passive voice.* Remember that your purpose as a military writer is neither literary nor diversionary but communicative.

Setting aside everything else, I favor the active voice because it saves readers time. It saves them time by being more direct (the doer is clearly visible) and by using fewer words. The difference in word count is, in large part, a function of the verb "to be." If that doesn't make sense, go to Part II and look up "passive voice." Here are a couple of dramatic examples showing the difference between the passive and active voices.

Passive: For about eighteen months, the program has been accomplished by in-house personnel in the operations center, all of whom have primary tasks other than the operations center upgrade. (29 words)

Active: For about eighteen months, in-house personnel, in addition to their primary tasks, have been carrying the operations center upgrade. (21 words)

Passive: Until the concept plan for the provisional agency is approved, the hiring of civilian personnel is precluded. In order to have financial programs in place at the start of the fiscal year, it is imperative that qualified programming and budgetary personnel be hired expeditiously. (44 words)

Active: Do not hire civilians until we approve the concept plan for the provisional agency. Hire qualified programmers and accountants quickly so that financial programs are in place when the next fiscal year starts. (33 words)

VOCABULARY

In those last two examples, had I done nothing but get rid of forms of the verb "to be," the revisions would have been longer. The fact is, I couldn't help myself from playing with vocabulary here and there. Vocabulary is an important aspect of style, and when it isn't good, neither are the reader's chances of understanding what you mean. Much of the reader's understanding hinges on clarity, and much of clarity hinges on vocabulary.

Virtually all style manuals urge writers to be clear and concise. In terms of vocabulary, that means writers should pick and choose the best possible words. Fine. What are the best possible words? It depends on the audience. The military writer's audience is a more or less known quantity. It consists of time-poor people who are driven by an abiding sense of mission and haunted by an unending requirement to come to terms with an incredible volume of electronic and printed writing. For such an audience, you want to use a vocabulary that will communicate what you have to say quickly and effectively.

Later in this chapter you'll find a list of vocabulary specifics, but for now, let's look at a few general rules that will help you develop a vocabulary that will serve both you and your reader efficiently. First, *use short words when it makes sense to use them.* By short words, I mean words of one or two syllables. Don't "indicate" when you can "show," don't "facilitate" when you can help, don't "promulgate" when you can "announce." If you want to improve your writing, get into the habit of stopping each time you use a word of more than two syllables and asking yourself, Do I know a short word that means the same thing? If the answer is yes, use that word.

Sometimes, though, a short word may not be the best choice. "Foe" is a case in point. Though only one syllable, it isn't often used in a modern military context. "Halt! Who goes there, friend or foe?" has been around for a very long time. And that's precisely my point. The word "foe" calls up images of thousands of Philistines moving into position. If you tell a soldier to close with the foe and destroy him, he'll wonder whether to use a rifle or the jawbone of an ass. The three-syllable "enemy" is a better choice because it is the more common word. That illustration makes the case for the second rule: *Choose familiar words that are commonly used today.*

It is possible, even using short and familiar words, to clutter your writing with words and phrases that you don't really need. But you can achieve economy of language if you follow this rule: *Avoid wordy transitional phrases that replace single words.* "In the event that" is a long-winded way of saying "if"; "for the purpose of" and "to" mean the same thing; and "in the near future" is another way to say "soon." Every now and then (that means the same thing as "sometimes"), you may want to use one of those kinds of phrases to produce a certain stylistic effect. Before giving in to that urge, keep in mind what you're doing: communicating with busy people who haven't time to indulge your muse.

I want to communicate with *you,* but you are a different kind of audience. And our context is different too. You, at least, came to this book more or less willingly and on your own time. The military people you write for don't come to your writing in the same way. They're in a hurry. Don't do anything to hold them up.

Redundancies will hold them up. In their desire to be understood exactly, many writers become redundant. Most of the time, though, redundant phrases puzzle those who have to figure out what they're supposed to mean. Military writers seem especially susceptible to being redundant.

Part of that susceptibility has to do with the tone of bureaucratic writing in general—it tries to be precise to a fault—and part simply reflects a fascination with the sound of certain phrases. There are thousands of them to pick from, but these show the error as well as any:

> Chief Petty Officer Bronson served well for an extended *time period.*

> The *end result* of this study was the purchase of the new bayonet.

> Private Fluellen violated his *contractual agreement* with the education center.

Each of these sentences has an extra word that adds nothing to our reading but time. Additionally, the extra word also makes the writing sound pompous. Without it, each sentence seems less stuffy:

> Chief Petty Officer Bronson served well for an extended *period.*

> The *result* of this study was the purchase of the new bayonet.

> Private Fluellen violated his *contract* with the education center.

A similar error is the use of the word "very" with an adjective or adverb expressed in the superlative degree, for example, very best, very dearest, very worst, and so on. If something is already best, another word or two won't make it better. You can't put ten gallons of water in a five-gallon tank. Don't try to force the issue with words either.

In like fashion, you must also avoid using "most" or "very" to intensify words that express absolute conditions. For instance, very pregnant, most unique, very last, very dead, and most final are all impossible constructions. If something is unique, it is not like anything else. That's what the word means: It is concerned with a state or condition, not a degree. Words such as "afraid" and "courageous" are relative; with them, "most" and "very" work fine. "Last" and "unique" are not relative terms. To treat them as if they were amounts to a logical impossibility. That's an error you want to avoid.

Choosing short words over long ones, using one word where you could have used four, and avoiding redundancy will save your reader a lot of time. So will using words in their best configurations. But what does that mean? Let's approach it by looking at the way our language allows us to turn perfectly good verbs into not-so-good nouns. The thing that makes them not so good is that when we use them, we need to use extra words. Look at these examples:

> The navigator *gave a demonstration of* the new radar unit.

> Lately the club board's *governance has been* poor.

> Major Brice *conducted his investigation* of the incident for days.

> The second brigade's plan *puts too much of a dependence* on the reserve battalion.

> In the future, do not *take your complaining* to the mess sergeant.

> The command group *had a discussion* about the new air defense system.

Many nouns ending with *-ance, -ence, -ing, -sion,* and *-tion* also exist, but in slightly different configurations than verbs. When you can use the verbs, by all means do. As a rule, it will save you words, and it will make your writing less mushy. Good, strong verbs have a hard-hitting quality that suggests that the person using them is in control, not only of the language, but of the situation as well. And that's never a bad secondary message to send to your reader. Look at the difference in these recast examples:

> The navigator *demonstrated* the new radar unit.

> Lately the club board *has governed* poorly.

> Major Brice *investigated* the incident for days.

> The second brigade's plan *depends too much* on the reserve battalion.

> In the future, do not *complain* to the mess sergeant.

> The command group *discussed* the new air defense system.

In a sentence of ten words, two or three words more or less won't make much difference, right? Perhaps. But what about in a paper of twenty such sentences? Now we're talking twenty to thirty words difference. And in a paper of a thousand words, it's the difference of a whole page—roughly a fourth of the total reading time.

Unless you have good reason to do otherwise, follow this rule: *Use verbs as verbs and nouns as nouns.* In the case of verbs, following that rule will make your writing both shorter and stronger. In the case of nouns, following it will keep you from looking like a boob. As far as English usage is concerned, there is nothing wrong with saying, "They had a discussion," instead of "They discussed." But as a comparison of the last two examples shows, it is poor style for a military writer.

Using words such as "caveat," "resource," and "interface" as verbs is not only poor style, but also poor usage. They are nouns, not verbs, and they shouldn't be used as if they were. No doubt, these examples will have a familiar ring to them:

> Before implementing this new plan, we need to *interface* with the next higher headquarters.

> Unless the fleet can *resource* this operation, we will have to drop it.

> Let me *caveat* my remarks with an observation.

In each of these sentences, the writer has improperly used a good noun to make a bad verb. Think back to the little quiz on words in chapter 3. Even when used properly, words are tough to understand; when used as they are in the example above, they put the reader's understanding at greater risk.

"Interface" is a noun that means a surface forming a common boundary. Which of the following does the writer of the first sentence mean?

> Before implementing this new plan we need to [form/recognize/have] a common boundary with the next higher headquarters.

> Before implementing this plan we need to [tell/coordinate with/get permission from] the next higher headquarters.

Probably, the writer had the second "translation" in mind. We can't be sure, though.

Likewise, the noun "resource" means an available supply, the ability to deal with a situation, or capital. The writer of the second sentence may be talking about people, materiel, ships, time, money, or none, some, or all those things. For the sentence to communicate, it needs a proper verb. For example:

> Unless the fleet pays for this operation, we must drop it.

The last sentence is even more confusing. "Caveat" comes into the English language from the Latin *caveat emptor:* "Let the buyer beware." The noun means a warning, but do we get that from the example? I read it to say:

> Let me preface [with reservations?] my remarks with an observation.

Maybe the writer wants it to say:

> Let me warn you about my remarks.

Who knows?

Military writers fall into the trap of using nouns as verbs because they think it makes what they write sound military. We've seen how confusing that can be for the reader. Beyond that, it's just foolish to try to express yourself that way. When the waiter gives you the tab, do you head for the cashier to "resource" it? Probably not. Don't do that kind of thing to your readers either. They are in the military, but they are also human beings who have the same problems with understanding that other mortals have. Do what you can to help solve them.

There is one thing you can do to short circuit a potential problem before it becomes one. The preface to this book notes the influence that so-called political correctness has had in our culture and, by extension, on our language. Don't ignore its force or its legitimacy. You can be linguistically and grammatically correct using this word or that and still get failing marks for style. If your rounds fall on a friendly force, all the self-vindicating technical correctness you might bring to bear cannot undo the damage. To borrow from Edward Fitzgerald's 1859 translation of The Rubáiyát of Omar Khayyám:

> The moving finger writes; and, having writ,
> Moves on: nor all thy piety nor wit
> Shall lure it back to cancel half a line,
> Nor all thy tears wash out a word of it.

Stay away from words that common sense ought to tell you are covered in red flags. "Niggard" comes to mind. A usage note for "niggard" in *The Encarta World English Dictionary* acknowledges the word's ultimate derivation from Latin and emphatically rules out its being a racial slur. The passage goes on to caution, however, "That the word sounds as if it might be one is reason to consider context very carefully before using it." Although "niggard," like "foe," is not a word most military writers would reach for, the example is instructive in any case because there are others. Often (and perhaps usually) perception has more force than reality. That's all the more reason to pay attention to what you're doing. In the best case, "niggard" will work against the writer who uses it because of the word's rarity, which means that the objective of having the writing understood in a rapid reading is undercut; in the worst case, it will cause friendly casualties.

A final point on vocabulary has to do with the specialized language and terminology common to the military. Every profession has a certain amount of it, but the military seems especially rich in jargon. New examples of jargon appear like weeds; and, like weeds, these new "words" have little real value and are hard to get rid of.

Military jargon takes too many forms for us to focus on more than a couple of them. One form is the use of several vague words to replace a single concrete one: "naval personnel" for "sailors," "field training exercise" for "maneuver," and "service personnel" for "soldiers," for example. Euphemisms—supposedly inoffensive terms used to replace offensive ones, for example, "police action" for "war" and "meeting engagement" for "fire fight"—themselves become a kind of jargon.

Incidentally, if you haven't read it already, make the effort to get hold of a copy of George Orwell's essay "Politics and the English Language." After reading what he has to say on the subject of fashioning neutral phrases to camouflage ugly truths, you'll find it difficult to do it yourself.

Words ending in *-ize* are a staple of martial jargon. Military writers love such words as "finalize" and "utilize"; they love such nonwords as "prioritize" and "soldierize". Somehow that *-ize* ending has an authoritative ring to it. "Finalize" sounds sharp, lean, tough—Prussian. Never mind that it means the same thing as "conclude," "end," and, for that matter, "make final." Sometimes military writers cannot escape using jargon. A site called a "maximum training area" never should have been named that in the first place. Is a "minimum training area" the base exchange? The gym? Your quarters? Foolish as that name is, to try and change it would probably do more harm than good. You could always consider calling it by its proper name: Camp Smith. Of course you may not have a choice. But when you do, use clear, short, and simple words instead of jargon. And use those words in clear, short, and simple sentences.

The next chapter deals with the kinds of sentences you may write. Before worrying too much about sentence variety, though, worry first about clarity. *Write sentences that communicate in the fewest number of words you can use without being rudely abrupt or brief at the expense of meaning.*

One way to do that is to write in the active voice. Another is to use the kind of vocabulary that will promote an understanding of what you have to say. Some of your sentences will have to be long and involved; there's no getting around that. But all of them certainly won't. In fact, most won't. Make it your goal to write sentences no longer than fifteen words. To do that, you need not lapse into a "run, Spot, run" mode. Nor must you write in telegraphic bullets. Short sentences and stupid writing are not the same thing. Just keep in mind that you have about fifteen words you can use to transmit a particular bit of information. Avoid trying to transmit bits so big that you can't manage them in fewer than thirty words.

Suppose you have a suitcase that will hold forty bricks. Fill it up, and you won't be able to lift the thing. Then what have you gained? Making ten loads of four bricks isn't the answer either. But three or four loads of about the same size will get the job done without hurting you or taking all day. That's true in military writing too.

TONE: FORMALITY VERSUS INFORMALITY

Though many things might be said about formality and informality, against a backdrop of trying to move paper quickly and efficiently, three seem particularly important: the use of personal pronouns, "please" and "thank you," and contractions.

Personal Pronouns

Unless someone forces you to do otherwise, use personal pronouns when you write as you would use them in normal speech. In *Hamlet,* the prince gets angry at one of his friends for referring to Gertrude as "your mother" instead of as "the queen." Hamlet's annoyance makes great sense in the context of Elizabethan England. It makes none today.

Certainly you want to observe the rules of decorum. A good way to do that is to worry less about showing respect and more about being polite. Being polite implies respect. Accept that, and write accordingly. In face-to-face conversation, most people would not ask Colonel Boswell, "Will the colonel accept the recommendation?" How stilted! Even Hamlet wouldn't go for that. And if that sort of discourse is bad orally, it's even worse in writing.

If a rule of thumb will help, try this one: *Use personal pronouns in military writing as you might use them in polite formal conversation.* Consider these three passages:

Last week our movement to Site X was approved subject to DOD funding. Funding has been approved by DOD. Movement can begin as early as next month. By the end of next month, movement of the unit must be accomplished. Recommendation: that the unit be moved as early as possible. (50 words)

Last week headquarters approved our movement to Site X subject to DOD funding. DOD has approved the funds. Movement can begin as early as next month. The unit must be at Site X by the end of next month. Recommendation: that movement of the unit occur as early as possible. (50 words)

I recommend we move to Site X as soon as possible. Last week you approved the movement subject to funding. DOD has approved the funds. We can be ready to move on the first of next month. We must be at Site X by the thirtieth. (46 words)

Length really isn't an issue, as all three passages have about the same number of words; however, tone is. The first example is passive; the second, stuffy; and the third, least stilted. Tone, you will recall from chapter 3, has an important place in the communicative process. In writing, tone is a function of style. One way to control it is by the way you use personal pronouns. In the end, it all comes back to something we took up earlier: judgment.

"Please" and "Thank You"

A second matter, also related to courtesy, is the use of "thank you" and "please." Those words seldom turn up in military prose. Perhaps they don't sound military enough; perhaps they don't seem to fit in with a system where rank can make things happen without them. Whatever the reasons, military writers rarely use "please" or "thank you." Instead, they crank out stuff that looks like the following:

Request attached draft be coordinated with principal staff sections.

Request your office review and provide comments by return e-mail.

Request favorable consideration of this request to relocate Battery B.

The headquarters appreciates your concern in this matter.

This is to indicate the commander's pleasure with the performance turned in by Sergeant Poins.

These sentences, beyond being stilted, use words they don't need. Rewritten, they are both shorter and more direct:

Please coordinate this draft with principal staff sections.

Please review and comment on this draft by return e-mail.

Please let Battery B move. Or: Please let me move Battery B.

Thank you for your concern in this matter.

Thank Sergeant Poins for his good work.

This is another area where you have to use common sense. Maybe this will help: In the imperative mood (that is, when you're giving orders), "please" and "thank you" get in the way. "Attention, please" isn't much of a command; neither is "ready, aim, fire . . . please." The "please" clutters those otherwise good sentences, which should tell you it doesn't belong.

On the other hand, if you find yourself reaching for the word "request," you most likely have a place for "please." In fact, over the years "request" has become a kind of military code for "please." Unlike "please," though, it cannot stand alone. What choices, then, does that leave the writer? Two come to mind: Either issue an order or directly face up to the need to ask nicely. In other words,

turn

Request you provide me with the information by Friday.

into

Give me the information by Friday.

or

Please give me the information by Friday.

What that really comes down to is being aware of your place relative to your audience. And as you know, that's something you need to be in control of before you write word one. Keeping your audience in mind, follow this rule of thumb: *Use "please" and "thank you" when they will enhance what you need to say.*

Contractions

A final point on formality has to do with contractions. Throughout this book I have used them freely, but not every time I could have. If I had, my last sentence would read, "Throughout this book *I've* used them freely, but not every time I *could've*." One look at that sentence should tell you why I haven't; yet it makes sense for me to write "haven't" where I just used it. This book is not a formal document. I have tried to write it in a somewhat more conversational tone than I would use in a scholarly monograph. I have also tried to be more formal than I would be in a letter to a close friend.

Frankly, I think this book has far more contractions than a formal military document ought to have. But I am trying to do more here than I would be if I were writing a military paper. First of all, my audience here is very broad; second, I don't want the tone of the book to be so high-blown that it turns people away; and third, a lot of people have trouble with the subject of writing, and I want what I have to say about it to be accessible to them. No, I want it to be more than that: I want it to be nonthreatening.

Whether this book helps you depends on a lot more than using contractions, but they are part of the equation. My guess is that I have used them in such a way that they contribute to the book's value rather than detract from it. My point? *Use contractions when they will help your reader get through your writing quickly and easily.* When they won't, don't use them.

As a rule, when writing for (or in the persona of) a flag officer, it's probably a good idea to be very careful with contractions. Don't be so careful, though, that you fail to use them when they really do fit. For writing below the flag level, you should be able to use contractions—indeed you *should* use them—fairly often in the interest of shortness and clarity. Some trite examples include the following:

Smoking on the bus is not permitted.

Don't smoke on the bus.

Eating in the theater is not allowed.

Don't eat in the theater.

Sometimes the unexpected appearance of a contraction can give a deadly dull piece of writing an emphatic lift. Compare the two passages below:

Currently, one action officer is assigned to accomplish the workload. The remaining manpower requirement is unresourced.

Now, one action officer must do the work. That's not enough.

In the matter of contractions, as in the broader matters of formality and informality, the proper measure depends on good judgment. Nothing succeeds like success, and you're apt to come pretty close to it if you avoid the extremes. Whatever their rank, age, station, interests, capabilities, skills, limitations, biases, strengths, or weaknesses, your readers are alike in one respect: They're all people. Keep that in mind as you write, and focus your efforts on making what you have to say understandable to them. If you do that, issues of formality and informality will take care of themselves with very little extra work on your part.

WORDS AND PHRASES TO AVOID

Many people expect military writing to sound a particular way, and when it doesn't, they get nervous. Let's go back a moment to the last examples about contractions. Anyone who uses "the remaining manpower requirement is unresourced" as a way of saying "we need more people" is not going to benefit from a list of words and phrases to avoid. If you think there's nothing wrong with "the remaining manpower requirement is unresourced" at this stage of things, then you need to go back to chapter 1. And if you really hate that phrase because it's pompous, wordy, overblown, self-aggrandizing, and uncommunicative, then you probably don't need a list of words to avoid.

But if you know you're *supposed* to hate it and really don't, then perhaps this list will have some value for you. It is not complete. It couldn't be—as soon as one offending phrase or word falls out of favor, two others seem to replace it. The point in including the list here is simply to illustrate the kind of language that defeats effective military communication and to show you some alternatives to it.

Avoid	Use
a number of	some, many, few
accomplish	do
accordingly	so
additional	further, more, other
advantageous	helpful, useful
and/or	and
appropriate	apt
as a means of	to
assistance	aid, help
at the present time	now
attention is invited to	note
authorize	allow, let, permit
caveat	warn, warning, caution
close proximity	near
comprise	make up
consequently	so
constitute	contain, include
contractual agreement	agreement, contract
contribute	give
currently	now
definitive	final
demonstrate	show
designate	assign, name
discontinue	end, stop
disseminate	pass out
due to the fact that	because
echelons	levels
eliminate	end, remove
enable	let
end result	end, result
enumerate	count, list
establish	make, set up, show
evaluate	test
expedite	hurry, speed
expeditious	fast, quick
facilitate	ease, make easier
finalize	conclude, end, finish

Avoid	Use
firstly	first
for the purpose of	for
give feedback	respond
have to	must, need to
hopefully	I hope
immediately	at once, now
in accordance with	under
in addition to	also, plus, too
in an effort to	to
in conjunction with	with
in order that	so
in regard to	to
in the course of	during, when
in the event that	if
in the near future	soon
in the recent past	lately, recently
in view of	since
inasmuch as	since
indicate	show
initially	first
initiate	start
input	data, thoughts
interface	connect, talk
it is important to note that	note
maximum	most
minimize	decrease, reduce
minimum	least
modify	change
more importantly	more important
most unique	unique
necessitate	cause, make, need
not later than	before, by
notify	tell
optimize	improve, strengthen
optimum	best
period of time	period, time
personnel	people

Avoid	Use
pertaining to	about
presently	now
previous	earlier
previously	before
prioritize	rank
promulgate	announce
provided that	if
request	please
requirement	need
secondly	second
selection	choice
subsequent	later
sum total	sum, total
the fact that	that
this point in time	now
time period	period, time
until such time as	until
utilization	use
utilize	use
very last	last
very least	least
with reference to	about
with the exception of	but, except

7

Correctness

The people you write for expect your writing to be generally correct. Whatever your weaknesses as a writer, you can still meet their expectations fairly easily if you master three things:

1. Spelling
2. Sentence construction
3. Subject-verb agreement

Get those things right and, no matter what other mistakes you make, your writing will be generally correct. Get them wrong and, no matter what else you do right, you leave your reader with the impression that you can't write—or worse, that you're dumb.   .

SPELLING

Let's get the easiest out of the way first. Spelling is something you absolutely must control. Your readers do not want to know about your chronic mental block when it comes to spelling, your disadvantaged background, or your history of dyslexia; they do not want a sheepish grin or hangdog look punctuated with embarrassed apologies. They just want you to write without gross spelling errors.

If you happen to be one of the relative handful of people with a problem such as those mentioned above, take the initiative to solve it, or find someone who can. Do not wait for a knock on your door or a telephone call: Help of the sort you're after does not intrude itself the way mutual fund brokers or insurance agents do.

Obviously, if you have a problem that needs special attention, ignoring it or hoping you can work around it makes no sense. The longer you hide it, the higher the stakes get, and all the more damaging its discovery can be.

If, on the other hand, your difficulties with spelling are less problematic and instead simply reflect some form of indifference, ignorance, or laziness, then their resolution comes down to two things: you and a speller.

Virtually all computer-based writing systems have programs that can make your spelling more or less error-free. However, if you use one of them, take care not to depend on it too much. Spell-check does have its limitations. You might type the phrase "fisical examination" and have it corrected to "fiscal examination," but if your focus is medical rather than financial, the phrase still has an error.

Make no mistake about it, over the last decade spell-check features have been responsible for broadly circulating and thereby accelerating the institutionalization of numerous spelling errors. "Led," the past tense of the verb "to lead," is spelled, more often than not, in newspapers, magazines, and television captions as the noun "lead" is spelled. Editors look at spell-checked copy, assume it is correct, print or post it, and make their daily contribution to the evolution (or devolution, depending on your point of view) of our language, as well as the conventions and rules that govern its use. The process is natural enough. English speakers have been able, over the seasons, to come to terms with a single spelling for the present and past tenses of the verb "to read." But there are still some readers who are not inclined to accept a single spelling for "lead" and "led." Because one or more of them may have occasion to read what you write, you would do well to know when to use one or the other.

Printed spellers—that is, alphabetized word lists—are a low-cost and utilitarian alternative to spell-check. They do not define the words they spell, though, and for all their utility, that's a clear disadvantage of using them. What's the point in spelling "compliment" correctly if you meant for the reader to understand it as "complement"?

In the absence of a fully loaded, impact-resistant laptop computer, you probably ought to consider using a dictionary as your primary resource for correct spelling. Which one? Any decent collegiate dictionary will do. And get a paperback version. Beyond being easier to use, the paperback dictionary weighs virtually nothing, travels well anywhere, and can be replaced for a few dollars.

How often you have to use the dictionary depends on what you do with the information you get out of it. If you mechanically copy a word you look up, you can plan on having to look it up the next time you want to use it. An alternative to that, of course, is to memorize the correct spellings of the words you look up. There's a short sermon on efficiency buried somewhere in all that, but those who already know how it goes shouldn't have to put up with it here; those who don't wouldn't pay attention to it anyway.

Whatever approach you take, you can count on one thing: Your readers will be intolerant of gross spelling errors. Though by no means acceptable, "accomodate" does not stigmatize the writer the way "recieve" does—at least not the first time. Of those two errors, the first seems merely ignorant (albeit embarrassingly so), but the second is gross because the word is common enough to appear in grade school spelling texts.

Don't, by the way, conclude that it's somehow all right to misspell some words but deadly to misspell others; instead, the moral here is that misspelling is unacceptable and should be treated with disdain, particularly since of all writing errors, it can be eliminated with the least difficulty.

SENTENCE CONSTRUCTION

Actually, the matter of sentence construction isn't difficult if you know and apply a few rules. Here's the most basic one: *Your readers expect you to write in complete sentences* (yes, occasionally someone will direct you to write using a kind of telegraphic or outline format, but probably not very often). Target your writing against that expectation, and ensure that you meet it. To do that, you need to follow one other rule: *Your sentence, to be a sentence, must have four things: a capital letter at its beginning, a subject, a verb, and a terminal punctuation mark.* Leave any one of those out and you don't have a sentence.

Of course, if you use nothing but those four elements, you're going to produce some tedious prose—so tedious, in fact, that your readers will not be much happier with you than they would have been had you written in something other than sentences. Sentence variety properly belongs under the heading of style, but it's nevertheless worthwhile to consider here. Basically there are four sentence structures:

1. Simple sentence
2. Complex sentence
3. Compound sentence
4. Compound-complex sentence

The grammatical units making up sentences are called clauses. Some of them are independent; some are dependent. Rather than labor over theory, consider these simple equations:

Simple sentence = independent clause

Complex sentence = independent clause + dependent clause

Compound sentence = independent clause + independent clause

Compound-complex sentence = independent clause + independent clause + dependent clause

The Simple and Complex Sentence

If the independent clause and the simple sentence are the same thing, then obviously the independent clause can function as a complete sentence. That means it has a subject and a verb; it may also have an object. (See Part II for more on all three.)

The dependent clause also has a subject and verb, and it may have an object as well. But unlike the independent clause, it cannot stand alone as a complete sentence. That's because the subject and verb of the dependent clause may not take the same form as those of the independent clause, or, when they do, some additional words will have changed the way they function.

Look at these examples:

1. Captain Jones saluted.
2. because Captain Jones saluted
3. that Captain Jones saluted

Note that the addition of the words "because" and "that" turns what were perfectly good sentences into *sentence fragments.*

Sentence fragments, though in some special circumstances quite effective, should not appear in your writing. Usually they bespeak incompetence, and you should avoid them. You already have two examples of sentence fragments, but let's define the error more precisely.

A sentence fragment is a clause or phrase lacking a subject or a verb, *or* one that fails to convey a complete thought or action. "Because Captain Jones saluted" has a subject of sorts (Captain Jones) and a verb (saluted), but it does not convey a complete thought. The same may be said of "that Captain Jones saluted."

Suppose that we add an object, in this case a direct object, to each of the examples. Will that change anything?

1. Captain Jones saluted Major Smith.
2. because Captain Jones saluted Major Smith
3. that Captain Jones saluted Major Smith

The answer, clearly, is no. The first example still is an independent clause *and* a complete, simple sentence. The remaining examples still are dependent clauses and sentence fragments.

At this point we need to consider two additional things: first, whether we can salvage the two sentence fragments; and second, whether we can convey a complete thought in the process. The answer is yes. But to do so, we have to use another kind of sentence: the complex sentence.

Here are a couple of possibilities:

> Because Captain Jones saluted Major Smith, the senior officer returned the salute.

> The report that Captain Jones saluted Major Smith proved true.

In the first example, the combination of the dependent and independent clause is straightforward; the dependent clause introduces the independent clause, or to say it another way, it provides an explanation of the complete thought: It tells us *why* the senior officer returned the salute.

In the second example, the dependent clause is sandwiched in the independent clause. "The report proved true" is a complete thought with its own subject and verb. By adding the dependent clause "that Captain Jones saluted Major Smith," we complicate things a bit grammatically (hence the term complex sentence), but, as in the first example, we explain or clarify something. In this case, we identify the nature of the report that proved true.

There's another common kind of sentence problem. Let's return for a minute to the first example:

> Because Captain Jones saluted Major Smith, the senior officer returned the salute.

The addition of the word "because" to an otherwise fine simple sentence (Captain Jones saluted Major Smith) got us to where we are now. Suppose we were to get rid of that word:

> Captain Jones saluted Major Smith, the senior officer returned the salute.

We no longer have a complex sentence, but instead, another gross error in sentence construction: a comma splice. The *comma splice,* as the term suggests, is the splicing together of two sentences with a comma when other punctuation or words must be used to connect them.

"Captain Jones saluted Major Smith" is a complete sentence; so is "the senior officer returned the salute." If you want to go a step beyond Dick-and-Jane sentence construction, you might consider either of these alternatives:

> Captain Jones saluted Major Smith; the senior officer returned the salute.

> Captain Jones saluted Major Smith, and the senior officer returned the salute.

On the other hand, sometimes the Dick-and-Jane approach may be the one to take:

> Captain Jones saluted Major Smith. The senior officer returned the salute.

Those are matters of style. The point to be made here is that the comma splice, like the sentence fragment, is an inexcusable mistake. And as you can see from the three correct alternatives, it's one you need not make.

Of the three examples, the third takes the form of two simple sentences: subject-verb-object and subject-verb-object. The other two are compound sentences.

The Compound Sentence

Compound sentences are made up of two or more independent clauses. Those clauses can be joined together in two general ways. One way, as the first example above shows, is with the semicolon.

Semicolons tend to be a little scary because most folks don't have a clue how to use them. Don't be put off by something that insignificant. There are lots of rules governing their use, but for our purposes here, you only need to know that in compound sentences semicolons may be used by themselves (as in the example above) or with a conjunctive adverb.

Conjunctive adverbs are nothing to be leery of either; indeed, you're already familiar with them. The term simply means adverbs that function as conjunctions (words that join independent clauses together). Here are a few of the more familiar ones:

therefore	accordingly	also
nevertheless	consequently	hence
moreover	still	indeed
however	furthermore	besides

Now here's the rule: *If you want to use one of these words to join the independent clauses of a compound sentence, you must precede the conjunctive adverb with a semicolon and follow it with a comma.*

If that's too much to remember, then don't use the conjunctive adverb; instead, use a semicolon by itself. You choose. (Keep in mind that the preceding chapter has already given you some guidance as to which choices you might want to make.) You may leave the sentence as it stands in the first of our three examples, or you may write it thus:

> Captain Jones saluted Major Smith; therefore, the senior officer returned the salute.

If that's the sentence you like, keep in mind that you had better have a pretty good reason for using it. Why? Because it's stuffy, perhaps to a fault. But for those occasions when you want to be stuffy (notice that I said "occasions" rather than "times" in keeping with the stuffy theme), at least you will know how to do it right.

A third, and probably the most familiar, alternative in constructing compound sentences is to use a coordinating conjunction. Coordinating conjunctions are words that bring together (or coordinate) elements of more or less equal grammatical rank—two independent clauses, for example. Below are some of the most common ones:

and	so	while
but	nor	or
yet	for	whereas

When you use a coordinating conjunction in a compound sentence, remember that you have to precede it with a comma. Remember, too, that not just any coordinating conjunction will work. Words such as "for" and "so" imply causal relationships, "but" suggests contrasts, and so on. Let's return to our example. "Captain Jones saluted major Smith, *and* the senior officer returned the salute" makes sense. Likewise, "Captain Jones saluted Major Smith, *so* the senior officer returned the salute" is also a decent sentence. "Captain Jones saluted Major Smith, *but* the senior officer returned the salute" is not, however.

By paying attention to those few rules, you will avoid the ignominy of producing fused sentences. They deserve the same scorn we have heaped on sentence fragments and comma splices.

The fused sentence, like the comma splice, is a variety of the run-on sentence. It is the joining together (or fusing) of two or more independent clauses without using coordinating conjunctions (or other coordination, such as conjunctive adverbs) or proper punctuation. For instance:

> Captain Jones saluted Major Smith the senior officer returned the salute.

Not writing a fused sentence of that sort should be easy enough. You may have to pay closer attention as your sentences expand, though. Consider this:

> Captain Jones saluted Major Smith, and the senior officer returned the salute he had no choice even though the captain someone he disliked annoyed him.

That example becomes a fused sentence, partially because its length makes controlling it harder, and also because the ideas it attempts to convey are more complex. Whatever the explanation, we're still left with a fused sentence, and that is unacceptable. Following the rules addressed above, we might recast it this way:

> Captain Jones saluted Major Smith, and the senior officer returned the salute; he had no choice, even though the captain, someone he disliked, annoyed him.

The Compound-Complex Sentence

In correcting the above sentence, we also produced a compound-complex sentence. The compound-complex sentence merely combines the elements of the complex and compound sentences. In the case of the example, there are three independent clauses:

> 1. Captain Jones saluted Major Smith

> 2. the senior officer returned the salute

3. he had no choice

and one (technically two) dependent clause:

1. though the captain [2. someone he disliked] annoyed him

These come together to form a single, grammatically correct, and fairly complicated sentence.

Compound-complex sentences have their place in military writing. When complicated ideas need expressing, use the best tools you have available. But use them prudently, and make sure you really need to use them. The object of the exercise should not be a bravura display of your verbal flourishes, but rather the production of material that your reader can understand in one fast reading. Most readers have to slow down to get through sentences like the one serving as our example.

SUBJECT-VERB AGREEMENT

Subject-verb agreement is the third thing you have to come to terms with for sentence correctness. You can overcome any difficulties you may have with subject-verb agreement—whether those difficulties reflect a disadvantaged background, bad grammatical habits, previous indifference, or simple ignorance—without undue hardship, if you'll learn a couple of rules and apply them with the same sort of self-discipline you customarily bring to other tasks you aren't excited about but know you must take care of nonetheless.

Rule 1: Some subjects are singular; some are plural.

Rule 2: Singular subjects need singular verbs; plural subjects need plural verbs.

That's it.

However, some words will fool you; you'll think they're singular because a lot of people use them that way, when in fact they're plural. Not knowing any better, you'll probably use singular verbs with them and wind up making an agreement error, such as "the *criteria* for approval *is* not clear" or "my *data is* incomplete."

Both "criteria" and "data" are plural forms; so are *media, strata, memoranda, phenomena, curricula,* and a lot of other similarly formed words. The less common ones—curricula, for example—probably won't cause you much trouble. But "data" and "media" might—until a new rule governing their usage develops. More and more, both words seem to be used as singular *and* plural nouns, in the same way we use the words "deer" and "fish." But words such as "criteria" and "strata" are not in any sort of usage transition, so with them you have to be especially careful.

"My data is incomplete," usage currency notwithstanding, is still incorrect. But the error isn't gross. "The criteria for approval is not clear," however, is still a gross error and one that causes the person making it to look like a boob.

Those concerns have ephemeral importance in the context of the more familiar language you work with most of the time. In that context, subject-verb agreement errors stand out like a leper in a nudist colony. Consider these examples:

> The squad of rangers were deployed.

> A box of grenades were lost.

> Four waterpoints needs to be established.

> She is one of those officers who has made a real contribution to the unit.

> Her bearing and fitness reflects great credit on the unit.

You can stay away from making these kinds of agreement errors by doing two things: first, know what your subject is; and second, determine whether it's singular or plural. The rest is easy.

In the first example, the singular noun "squad" is the subject. It must have a singular verb:

> The squad of rangers *was* deployed.

The same applies to the next example. "Box," the singular subject, takes a singular verb:

> A box of grenades *was* lost.

In the next example, the plural subject "waterpoints" demands a plural form of the verb:

Four waterpoints *need* to be established.

The next example is a little trickier than the others because it is a complex sentence. In sentences such as this one, *the number of the subject* (that is, whether the subject is singular or plural) *of the relative clause dictates the number of the verb.* Let's look at the example again:

She is one of those officers who has made a real contribution to the unit.

In this example the relative clause is "who has made a real contribution to the unit." The subject of that clause is "who." The antecedent of the subject—that is, the "who" being talked about—is "officers." That means that "who" is plural. If the subject is plural, you know it takes a plural verb. In this case, that verb is "have." Correctly written, the example now reads like this:

She is one of those officers who *have* made a real contribution to the unit.

The last example also requires a plural verb form. Bearing and fitness are two nouns that *together* function as a plural subject:

Her bearing and fitness *reflect* great credit upon the unit.

As you should expect, occasional exceptions will crop up to complicate things. For instance, based on the way we treated bearing and fitness, you might be tempted to write:

Ham and lima beans are a meal the troops dislike.

Wrong. In this case, "ham and lima beans" combine to make a collective thought (the name of a particular dish), and the rule is: *A collective thought functioning as the subject of a sentence takes a singular verb.* Used in the sense of the example, ham and lima beans get lumped together.

On the other hand, those same nouns might be used as "bearing" and "fitness" were in the second example:

Ham and lima beans *are* two nutritious foods.

Why? Because here we're talking about two different things that belong to a larger category—in this case, food—as opposed to two things that collectively make up a particular meal.

To carry this a step further, many of the troops who hate ham and lima beans probably like ham and lima beans. Clearly, we're talking about two different things here: a meal and two foods.

You can make other kinds of agreement errors—pronoun-antecedent errors, for instance. Over the last several years, a sustained and conscious effort to eliminate gender-based language, especially in the workplace, has made statements such as "A soldier must plan their time carefully" commonplace in spoken American English. As the process of neutralizing pronouns in speech becomes increasingly common, it will also become increasingly acceptable and, in time, correct. Eventually, we will come to regard a person who resists such usage as someone who needs *their* head examined. Indeed, fewer and fewer people find anything wrong with the usage in a statement such as "The media is often tough during press conferences, but if a commander answers questions carefully, they can survive."

The currency and growing acceptance of such constructions can make the argument for correctness a hard sell. In practical terms, if a communication's correctness gets in the way of rapid reading, it also gets in the way of its effectiveness. Stated correctly—"The media are often tough during press conferences, but if a commander answers questions carefully, he can survive"—this sentence would puzzle some readers and anger others. What's the point of doing either? The writer's task is neither to baffle nor to irritate, but rather, to communicate effectively. Don't be a jerk just to make a point that many of your readers would miss anyway. Use judgment.

If the usage of our language is susceptible to occasional changes, most take effect pretty slowly. That means the majority of the old rules governing subject-verb agreement aren't going anywhere; neither are the old expectations of your readers. Quite simply, to produce the kind of generally correct writing your readers expect and deserve, you need to eliminate subject-verb agreement errors. And when you reasonably can, you ought to make it point to avoid pronoun-antecedent errors. Part II of this book has some material in it that will help you do that.

Spelling. Sentence construction. Subject-verb agreement. Though not mastered without a degree of study, practice, and self-discipline, these three will haunt you if you can't manage them correctly when you write. The modest amount of effort you bring to such mastery seems a small investment against the returns it will certainly produce.

8

Military Formats

Specific formats for different documents vary from service to service. Military formats, like other elements of communication, change with the personalities, missions, technologies, and capabilities they exist to support. One thing does not change, however: The people who must read the writing done in those various formats are overwhelmed by volume and short on time. Given that reality, you must make sure that your writing, in whatever format, responds to the task consciously and conscientiously. It's your duty.

What I am going to say in the balance of this chapter supposes several things. Foremost, it acknowledges the necessity for, and assumes your commitment to, writing things that can be understood in one fast reading. Second, it supposes that you have the fundamental skills in English usage, grammar, and mechanics you need to produce writing that is generally free of gross errors.

If these suppositions don't jibe with what you know to be reality, then we are at an impasse. That leaves you with a couple of clear choices. You can toss this book in the trash and go on to other things, or you can go back to the beginning and give it another try.

I should say that if you are not altogether confident about your skills with usage, you do have Part II as a reference. It's not the kind of material you can read through and absorb at one sitting. No doubt you'll have to come back to it from time to time. Consult it as often as you must.

GENERAL GUIDELINES
You know from reading chapter 5 that you can go a long way toward getting organized in the absence of an aim or purpose. But you also know that you must not start writing until you know the end to which your writing is directed. So the first step is clear: *Identify your aim.* And don't make this crucial process a private one either.

If you know you have significant obstacles between you and your reader—intermediate readers, your supervisor, other staffers—get them to concur in your aim. That may take some legwork and more than a little talking. The talking isn't a bad thing, though, particularly if it forces you to reexamine your own position critically, and perhaps even to change it slightly in the interest of getting everyone between you and the boss to embrace it. Here's the point: *Make sure that the intermediaries between you and your reader agree with your aim.*

KINDS OF FORMATS

Having done those things, you must *select the format that best suits your material and aim.* In many cases, the selection will have been taken out of your hands long before you get the assignment; indeed, it may come to you as "I need a memorandum on such and such." Even if the format does come to you with the assignment, before you begin writing, be sure material and aim really fit it. If they don't, then ask to change to a different one.

When formats aren't explicitly directed by someone, or a function of the requirement (for example, an award citation, a report of survey, etc.), the choice is up to you. For the sake of simplicity, you're better off staying away from the pronounced formality of letters. The *memorandum* is a flexible format that can serve virtually all the ends of a letter without being stuffy.

Whether your aim is information or persuasion, the memorandum format will accommodate you. Use memoranda to answer questions, update information, make recommendations, report findings, obtain decisions, and record significant events. Your memoranda should have headings, which flow from the brainstorming you do beforehand.

No matter what those headings turn out to be, get in the habit of making your first one "Purpose," unless you are constrained or directed otherwise. Then, in a short sentence, explain why you're writing the memorandum. Your next heading, depending on what you're trying to do, might be "Conclusion" (question), "Status" (information), "Recommendation" (recommendation), "Finding" (report), or "Result" (record). This second heading introduces your bottom line. All the other headings in the memorandum should be logically arranged to show how you got to it. Thus the memorandum amounts to little more than a description of your thought process.

In some contexts, an *information paper* can be particularly useful. As its name suggests, an information paper exists to inform. The title or subject of an information paper identifies it for what it is. There's no need to begin by giving the reader a statement of purpose, since purpose is obvious by definition. Your first heading, then, might (and probably should) be "Status."

Follow that heading with a one-sentence summary of what the paper says. The headings that come next should give an orderly picture of your brainstorming and any research it led you to do. Papers of this sort have a lot of uses. For example, they can turn out to be valuable enclosures to a memorandum.

Decision papers exist to persuade. Don't make the mistake of offering your reader several choices without the benefit of your recommendation. That recommendation, clearly, should follow your first heading. (Of course, if the title of the paper makes it pointless to have a first heading, don't have one.) Call the heading that introduces your bottom line either "Conclusion" or "Recommendation." Arrange your other headings, the results of your brainstorming and research, in such a way as to give the strongest support to your bottom line.

A *talking paper* or point paper can be used to inform or persuade. Depending on the user's purpose, prepare it as an abbreviated version of either an information paper or a decision paper. In that abbreviation, keep the same progression of headings I have already suggested. Except for a statement of the bottom line and the headings themselves, everything else could probably be cut without risk.

This abbreviated format assumes that the person using the talking paper already has some background in the subject at issue; it also assumes some ability with oral expression. On that basis, then, the talking paper is little more than a "cue card" for someone who has the script more or less memorized.

Talking papers should be to the point, crisp, and short. For a talking paper, a whole page is probably too much. Some people prefer to use a three-by-five card or two. If what you come up with won't fit on a couple of cards, you probably haven't produced a talking paper. And you certainly don't know your subject as well as you should.

Whatever format you settle on, don't make the unfortunate mistake of trying to use it to inform and persuade at the same time. If what you write happens to produce that effect coincidentally, fine. But let that be a happy accident, not something you consciously try to engineer. What I'm talking about here is a unity error. If you have two aims, you need two documents.

STEP-BY-STEP APPROACH

Format aside, as soon as you reveal the document's purpose, announce the *bottom line.* Your conclusion or recommendation should be the first thing you give your reader. Bottom lines can take many forms. Here are a few examples:

Limited space lets us add only eight more beds for inpatients.

You should approve the transfer of all airborne soldiers to the battalion's letter companies.

We have an effective system of retirement counseling in this command.

Chief Rostowe has performed superbly throughout the rating period.

Do not move the ammunition trains assembly area.

Specialist Fourth Class Wolfgang L. Sasson, 111-22-3333, is awarded the Army Commendation Medal for exceptionally meritorious service.

The division's forward tactical operations center will be located near LaVille, at RR09233675.

Except when writing citations and certain narratives (e.g., fitness reports), you should be able to *arrange your information under clear, logical headings.* On those rare occasions when you can't use the organizing device of headings, you can still proceed in an orderly and logically connected fashion. Review the steps in chapter 5 if you're not sure how to do that.

Most writing courses offered in an academic setting require the people who take them to compose fairly long paragraphs. Short paragraphs, many teachers might argue, are evidence of undeveloped ideas. An idea that's fully developed ought to fill up half a page, right? In some contexts, yes. But in the military, long, dense paragraphs are not desired.

A long paragraph containing the same number of words as three short ones should take no longer to read. It does, though. That's because busy readers are put off by anything that looks like it has a lot of words packed into it. This is another lesson in packaging: *Keep your paragraphs short—no longer than seven or eight single-spaced lines.* Show your reader a little blank paper from time to time. The result will be considerably less intimidation and faster reading.

If that seems to reflect a human limitation, it's because it does. Respond to it by feeding the reader chewable bites. You can certainly eat an apple that has been quartered faster than you can eat a whole one. And you can do it with a lot more grace. Whether quartered or whole, the apple is still the apple. So, too, with your writing. Package it to move.

If a dense paragraph intimidates a reader, what reaction will a document several pages long produce? That's the kind of document readers put back in their inboxes and consciously avoid until somebody puts something else or sends another e-mail message on top of it. Such a document may languish there for days until one night it finally makes the long journey home in a too-full briefcase or still-warm laptop. Small wonder that readers feel put upon.

Do everything in your power to *limit your base document to one page.* Many times you will need to deal with more material than a page will hold. When that happens, include the extra material in annexes, tabs, enclosures, appendices, or any other add-on format that your service's correspondence guidelines permit.

Putting the essential information on a single page is not as difficult as it may seem. An editor of only modest skill could still reduce the Normandy invasion plan to a base document of something less than a page. The balance of the document might be a foot thick, but its essence would be immediately available to the reader.

In assembling your supporting documents, be sure to *enclose any additional material in a logical and orderly manner.* Your enclosures should complement the various headings you use in the base document. They should not appear to be a glorified postscript to it.

Once you have written the one-page base document and assembled any enclosures, you will be in possession of a pretty decent hard-copy draft. *Show your draft to officemates,* and ask them to check its usage—especially spelling, agreement, and sentence structure—and logical flow. And after you've done that, you might subject your draft to a grammar check in your word processing program.

Make any changes or corrections, and *circulate your second draft to concerned intermediaries.* Whether you do that electronically or manually should be a matter of SOP within your office or unit. Either approach is going to cost you some time, but that goes with the assignment.

On the draft's return to you, *respond to any additional corrections or changes.* Once you have done that, you can *prepare the final copy, proof it, and send it forward.*

What you should notice about this process is that a good deal of the staffing can be informal. Throughout the process, rely as much as you can on personal visits and the telephone. The object of doing things in this somewhat informal way is to avoid going through the double and triple work of producing multiple versions of your drafts. Coordination by computer might be faster in the short term, but can you imagine what a mind-deadening exercise it would be to sift through a half-dozen or more electronic attachments of the same file for changes?

No doubt electronic coordination is highly efficient, but it may not always be the most effective way to staff your work. Remember the advice in chapter 3. Whether read from a piece of paper or a computer screen, writing is still writing. Resolve as many trouble spots as you can by using more effective means of communication: face-to-face conversation and the telephone.

SUMMARY

As should be obvious to you by now, this discussion can be reduced to a few specific suggestions that will help you approach military formats in a deliberately efficient manner. They are as follows:

1. Identify your aim.
2. Make sure that you and the intermediaries between you and your reader agree with your paper's stated aim.
3. Select the format that best suits your material and aim.
4. Start with a clear announcement of the purpose of your paper.
5. Follow that announcement with a forceful statement of the bottom line.
6. Arrange your information under clear, logical headings.
7. Keep your paragraphs short—no longer than seven or eight single-spaced lines.
8. Limit your base document to one page.
9. Enclose any additional material in a logical, orderly manner.
10. Show your draft to your officemates, and ask them to check its usage and logical flow.
11. Conduct a computerized check of your usage.
12. Circulate your second draft to concerned intermediaries.
13. Respond to any additional corrections or changes.
14. Prepare the final copy, proof it, and send it forward.

FORMAT EXAMPLES

As you look at these examples, don't focus on differences between the formats you know and the samples you see here. And don't worry about the content of the examples themselves. Instead, concentrate on the writing and its organization, style, and tone.

EXECUTIVE SUMMARY

Executive Summary for: CINCEUR
Subject: Possible Changes to Scheduled Base Transfers

1. *Purpose.* This paper summarizes time-sensitive reports (attached) prepared by the Army, Navy, and Air Force installation coordinators.
2. *Recommendation.* Direct the theater commander of each service to submit, by 26 August, a revised plan for sequenced base closing and transfer of facilities to host nations (proposed report format, Encl. 1).
3. *Summary.* These reports argue strongly for keeping open some of the bases this command has announced would close by the end of the next fiscal year. Each report makes its case on the recent instability in the Middle East; each also assumes that any bases the command decides to retain must still close by the end of the decade. In all cases, installation coordinators have urged short-term retention of the bases in question. A table outlining the recommendations of the three services (Encl. 2) highlights the general agreement of all reporting commands.
4. *Red Flags.* The possibility of delaying the scheduled closure and prompt release of some particularly desirable bases raises at least three red flags:
   - Budgetary impact
   - Tactical utility
   - Political backlash

Note: Enclosure 1 requires the reporting services to address all three in detail.

MEMORANDUM

Memorandum for: Lt Cmdr Shadwell
Subject: Creation of a NATO Service Medal

1. *Conclusion.* I agree that the Defense Department should create a NATO Service Medal.
2. *Discussion.* I do not believe, however, that your memorandum (Subj: as above, dtd 4 May) offers enough justification for the creation of this award. You speak of operations in potentially hostile environments and military risks, but you give little concrete information on either. Nor am I clear on whether such an award would include NATO service during which no hostile action takes place.
 Please suggest a design for the medal itself and for the ribbon as well.
3. *Tasks.* Specifically, if you want to proceed with this proposal, you should:
    a. Clarify the criteria for the award.
    b. Add the detail you need to make the case convincing.
    c. Develop a design for the medal and ribbon.
    d. Write a brief explanation of the thinking behind the design.
4. *Follow-up.* Let me know if you still want to make this proposal. Questions? Call Lt. Oates.

> John Dryden
> Capt., USN
> Commanding

DECISION PAPER

Decision Paper for: Lt. Col. Andre
Subject: Use of Battery Commanders as Staff Duty Officer

1. *Recommendation.* Direct the sergeant major to exclude battery commanders from his roster for staff duty officer effective 31 July.
2. *Discussion.* All company-grade officers serve as staff duty officer on a rotating basis. Depending on the rotation, each spends one or two nights a month away from home. The five battery commanders already spend the equivalent of three nights a week away from home. The battery commanders are in garrison most evenings; the other officers are not.

Two issues emerge from this discussion:
   a. Morale. The morale of the five commanders and their families will improve if you accept the recommendation.
   b. Fairness. The other officers recognize the burdens of battery command. None is likely to resent a relief of commanders from this duty.
3. *Courses of Action.* You have at least three courses of action:
   a. Continue the status quo.
   b. Exempt battery commanders from serving as staff duty officer on an experimental basis for two months.
   c. Exempt battery commanders from serving as staff duty officer.

> T. Everett Susato
> Capt., USMC
> Commanding

TALKING PAPER

Talking Paper for Meeting with LTG Jason, 19 April
Subject: Reviving the 47 (Education) Specialty

1. *Conclusion.* The Army's growing need for a group of professional educators argues for immediate revival of the 47 Specialty.
2. *Comment on Needs:*
   a. Academy faculties (USMA, USMAPS)
   b. Academic courses (history, writing, etc.) in Army schools
   c. Curriculum development (TRADOC)
   d. ROTC faculty
   e. Professional ethics instruction
   f. Think tanks
   g. Writing pools
3. *Cost Effectiveness?* Compare costs of in-house expertise vs. outside consultants (two charts, three transparencies).
4. *Disadvantages.* (Note: Ask whether these designations will continue, and then show chart of disadvantages.)
5. *Advantages.* (Note: Show chart of advantages first, and then stress value of in-house credibility.)

EVALUATION REPORT NARRATIVE

During the rating period, Sergeant Wagner outperformed every junior NCO in the company. His squad set the standard that other squads aspired to reach. In the field, his soldiers showed their mastery of infantry tactics: Their individual and unit test performances earned the squad the Brigade Commander's Trophy. In garrison, these same troops are the model of decorum. They take better care of their vehicles and equipment than any other unit on post. Under Sergeant Wagner's leadership, their performance is superb. This fine NCO is a natural leader who enjoys the respect of the whole company.

AWARD CITATION

Sergeant Hollis W. Wagner, 321-32-1321, is awarded the Army Achievement Medal for exceptionally meritorious achievement from 27 March through 15 May. When Sergeant Wagner became a squad leader, the soldiers under him were infamous for their poor training and misconduct. Working sometimes as long as sixteen hours a day, he turned them into masters of small-unit tactics. His squad received the Brigade Commander's Trophy for excellent test results. Under his leadership, the squad has become a well-disciplined fighting unit. Achievement of that sort is the hallmark of an outstanding leader. It reflects great credit on him, his unit, and the United States Army.

Postscript

In the preceding examples, I have not, by design, tried to stick to a particular approved format or to be especially realistic. I have, however, made an effort to model a style and tone that should fit in with any format, service notwithstanding. Good baseball players move easily enough between the National and American leagues and are effective in both. Never mind that each league has its own rules; good baseball is what matters.

9

Briefings
and Oral Presentation

Although this book is a guide for writers, much of what it has to say applies to speakers as well. How much? Almost all of it. Speaking and writing are the subsets within the larger verbal set. Approach an oral requirement as you would a written one. Bring to bear the same skills, the same sensitivity to the needs and endurance of your listener (as opposed to reader), and you will do well—at least as far as the product itself is concerned. With the exception of some comments on visual aids, nothing I say in this chapter is going to help you with delivery. That aspect of oral presentation is a subject for a separate book.

Few people in military service progress very far in the ranks before they find themselves in the business of making oral presentations. They come in all sizes and are directed to a broad range of ends. Whether repeating general orders learned by rote or extemporaneously exhorting an exhausted crew to fight on, people in the military cannot escape oral presentation. However obvious the point, it still seems worthwhile to say something about the kind of oral presentation that virtually all military people wind up making from time to time: *the briefing.*

Some briefings are long and complex, some short and simple; some formal, some not; some to inform, some to persuade; and so on. But most have a couple of things in common. First, because the briefing is a live, oral presentation, it demands tight organization. Second, because it is interactive, it depends on the briefer's having a particularly good command of the subject matter—to say nothing of the good sense simply to reply "I don't know" when he or she doesn't.

The immediacy of a live presenter and a live audience, of course, has both positive and negative implications. If you do your homework, pitch well, and keep your cool when questioned or challenged, you can step off the platform a hero; fail in any one of those, and you'll walk away a bum.

From time to time you may find yourself briefing someone who takes obvious pleasure in tormenting briefers. You know the type, and if you don't, you will. This person is an ulcer maker with an extensive collection of wingless flies. Nothing in this book can protect you from someone of that ilk, but some of the things in it may well help you engage in a little proactive damage control before the fact.

Fear not: The overwhelming majority of people you brief will listen supportively to what you have to say if they realize that you have put your presentation together with their needs in mind. And they will come rapidly to that realization if you bring to your oral delivery the same sense of purpose and businesslike lucidity that should already be a hallmark of your writing. Indeed, you should approach the preparation and presentation of a briefing in the same spirit and with the same professional discipline you bring to writing assignments.

Here, then, is a short primer for preparing a *briefing.* Begin by advising your audience of the *briefing's classification* (e.g., This is a secret briefing, etc.) and announcing its *purpose* (e.g., to obtain a decision as to the configuration of Task Force Red, to provide an update on the maintenance status of tankers in Sector Zulu, etc.) clearly and concisely. Whether briefing to persuade or inform, you need to have a firm sense of where you want the briefing to go.

Your *bottom line,* announced up front, will give you (and your audience) that firm sense of direction. If you say something such as "Our best intelligence analysts remain convinced that Task Force Red will need at least one additional carrier and two destroyers to make a dent in the enemy's present advantage," you can get about the business of showing your audience that your bottom line is no mere assertion. Your object is to have, at briefing's end, the boss's blessing on the configuration of Task Force Red, or at least some strong guidance as to the shape it must take.

Announcing the bottom line early on gives focus to informational briefings as well. You may not make the boss happy with the content of a bottom line such as "Maintenance of the tankers in Sector Zulu is at an all-time low, but the inspectors say that within the next thirty-six hours, all but one will be ready to fly." But you will, in any case, set a course for it to follow.

If the rationale for your bottom line involves several propositions, it is often useful to tell that to your audience, such as "There are four aspects to this question. The first is . . ."

How you keep it on that course depends on a number of variables.

Some people use a lot of *graphics.* If you are inclined in that direction, proceed with moderation. Often with graphic aids, and especially with overhead transparencies (no matter how slick or colorful), *less is more. Computer-supported presentations* have become increasingly commonplace and grow more sophisticated by the day. Dramatic fades in and out, sound effects, music, real-time video, and any number of similar bells and whistles make presentations of this sort dangerously seductive.

Be very careful here. All the special effects in the world will not make up for thinness of substance. Given a choice, I would rather be criticized for pitching a routine briefing of substance than for being the ringmaster of an insubstantial circus of pyrotechnics. People want the briefings they sit through to bring them up to date and provide contexts for their decisions and actions. If a computerized presentation can promote that end without being intrusive in itself, great; if not, look for another approach. One is reminded of Hamlet's mother, who, after a royal counselor has dazzled her with yet one more of his extravagant rhetorical flourishes without giving her anything of substance, acidly chides, "More matter, with less art."

Whatever approach you settle on for a particular briefing, keep in mind that it is seldom a good idea to turn the lights out on your audience; and it's almost never a good idea to keep lights out for very long. True enough, a picture is worth a thousand words. Some pictures, a good *map,* for instance, may be worth even more. Select yours with care, and if possible, use them as visual cues for your presentation.

No doubt you will want the feeling of security that having some kind of script in hand provides, but you would do well to keep anything you write to a minimum. The format of the *talking paper* (illustrated above) should serve you pretty well. After making clear the bottom line, you need to offer a detailed *statement of the problem or situation.* That statement should include both *assumptions* (e.g., The repair parts we need will be on hand by Friday) and *facts* (e.g., We cannot operate our tracked vehicles for longer than four minutes without damaging them) bearing on the briefing subject. It should also include, particularly in a decision briefing, an indication of the *courses of action* available and an analysis of the *advantages and disadvantages of each.* With that much presented, you then return to the bottom line you offered at the beginning and prepare to respond, as best you can, to questions and comments from the audience.

This book, as the remarks introducing this discussion emphasized, is not about oral presentations any more than it is about how to prepare a particular kind of document. Rather, it is about effective *verbal* communications, especially those you are forced to write down in some form. Most people, though, usually do at least roughly script their briefings on paper. You may be one of them, and if you are, think of this postscript as a discussion of another writing format. Careful: Don't let the word "script" tempt you to produce a full-blown text. Master the material you need to brief on, think it through, and organize it in a talking paper, a format that, as already noted, will be script enough.

10

General Formats

Most of the writing you do will be for a military audience. From time to time, though, you may find yourself writing for an altogether different group of readers. The prospect of doing that might make you a little nervous at first, but it need not. There's no reason why a good military writer can't communicate effectively with an audience outside the military.

A lot of people think that the military uses one kind of writing and the rest of the world uses something else. In one sense, that's true. When the military lapses into the passive voice, jargon, strings of acronyms and abbreviations, and obscure ten-dollar words, it is in a class by itself. But as more military writers have become conscious of those enemies of quick and effective communication, that kind of writing appears less frequently.

Even so, many people still think that the military and the rest of the world are at odds when it comes to writing. And they're right—sort of. The folks who think that way primarily tend to be the people who entered the military out of school or college. In those environments, the cast of writing is decidedly academic.

Academicians use long words, long sentences, and long paragraphs. For them, that kind of writing becomes almost an art form unto itself. They don't worry about having their stuff understood in one fast reading. On the contrary, they expect their readers to study what they write at some length.

It is not surprising that the academicians who teach writing would urge their students to write longer sentences, paragraphs, and papers. Nor is it surprising that people coming to the military on the heels of that kind of instruction would think military writing, even good military writing, is vastly different from what they're used to. It is.

But so is the writing of the corporate world. If the business of business is business, writing is simply a tool. To be a worthwhile tool, it must serve business in precisely the same ways it must serve the military. That is, it must transmit information in a form that a busy reader can understand in one fast reading. That means the bottom line must be up front, sentences must be around fifteen words long, paragraphs must not exceed seven or eight lines, and the base document must be no longer than a page.

All that leads to this point: *Good military writing does not differ from good writing in most other walks of life.* Except for academic, theological, and legal writing, what passes for good military writing will pass as good writing in any context. That being the case, you can confidently apply the principles and techniques in this book to most general formats.

As an aside, I should add this brief remark: Academics, theologians, and lawyers are no less interested in effective communication than the next person. And much of what this book says applies to their writing as well. If they must apply it in different ways, that's a function of audience. The difference, I would argue, has considerably less to do with brains than with the availability of time.

When you use general formats such as the ones treated in the balance of this chapter, you will be fairly safe in assuming an audience much like the one you write for in the military—readers who are generally intelligent, very busy, and usually overwhelmed by the amount of written material they deal with every day.

Writing for a general audience, you can count on a lot of tough competition. It is extremely important for you to make what you have to say accessible. One obvious way to do that is to write so that your reader does not have to slow down to make sense out of your writing.

You can also increase your writing's accessibility by making it look good on the page. In that regard, computers help a great deal. And they save a lot of time (to say nothing of heartburn) by making your work easy for a reader to edit and relatively painless for you to correct. Personal computers have become so common in the workplace and the home that readers have gotten used to the copy produced on them; indeed, they expect it. Even printers of poor quality spew forth documents that look as good or better than what was professionally printed a decade ago. And a color laser printer makes even drivel look great. It won't make it *be* great, of course, or even marginal, but if what you write falls out somewhere near the midpoint on the drivel-greatness scale, having it look good will enhance its chances of keeping it in front of your readers, if not actually communicating with them.

If chapter 8 only scratched the surface of military formats, this one offers even fewer examples of general formats. Their main purpose is to illustrate the sort of tone and organization that will make your writing communicate effectively in contexts beyond the military.

While you remain on active duty, most of your writing for audiences outside the military will be in letter form. For that reason, most of the examples that follow are letters.

BUSINESS LETTER

October 22, 2003

Mr. Ambrose Figgins
Credit Department
Allworthy Books, Ltd.
6 Xenon Boulevard
New York, New York 10021

Dear Mr. Figgins:

Shortly after the end of the month you should receive a $27 money order from Robert G. Wendig. Your letter of October 6 stated that Private Wendig (acct. 7223-A4) had not made his scheduled payments in three months. His money order will not cover the balance of those missed payments. It will, however, show his good faith and intention to pay his account in full. From a recent conversation with him, I am convinced that he intends to make the remaining payments on schedule.

Thank you for your concern.

Sincerely,

James B. Hook
Captain, USA

LETTER OF APPLICATION

September 15, 2003

Professor Anne T. Warden
Director of Graduate Studies
Department of Political Science
Blue Ridge University
Skyline, Virginia 28330

Dear Professor Warden:

I am applying for graduate admission to the Department of Political Science. Following the instructions of the Graduate School of Arts and Sciences, I have asked Educational Testing Service to forward copies of my GRE scores. They will come directly to you, as will my undergraduate transcript from Arlington University and letters of recommendation from three of my former professors.

With this letter I have enclosed the completed application forms. I have also enclosed six postcards. Each is stamped, addressed, and functionally labeled. Please drop the one labeled "application form" in the mail when you finish this letter. I should be grateful if you would forward the others as you receive my scores, transcript, and recommendations.

I understand that you announce your decisions by December 1. Should you need any information from me between now and then, please let me know. Thank you for your interest and consideration.

Sincerely,

Sven P. Larsen

Encls.

LETTER OF RECOMMENDATION

January 6, 2003

Mr. Pearson G. Wylde, Principal
East Valley Academy
Big Tree, California 96660

Dear Mr. Wylde:

I am pleased to recommend Elizabeth R. Lester for the Big Tree Chamber of Commerce Citizenship Award. This young woman is a vital and contributing member of this community.

Our first meeting occurred two years ago. You may recall that our Army reserve unit was controlling the valley's fire relief operations. The command post was scarcely functioning before Elizabeth appeared from nowhere and asked how she might help. Convinced she would get bored and leave, I gave her a few errands. She wound up working not only all day, but all summer.

That same spirit of public service reveals itself in her work as a volunteer aide at St. Mark's Hospital. She began her third year of service there in September. And it was Elizabeth who thought of sponsoring a race to earn money for the rescue squad's new van.

Her grades are quite good, too. Of course you already know that. You also know that she is active in drama club and chorus. No doubt you are aware that she is captain of the girls' soccer team this year.

Elizabeth Lester strikes me as the walk-away candidate for this important award. She has done much to deserve it.

Sincerely,

Margarette C. Narro

RESUMES

I am not going to offer a fully developed example of a resume; there are plenty of books on the market and in libraries with samples of resumes.[1] And there are a number of plug-and-chug software packages you can use. What I will offer, though, are some comments about how to organize them and a few thoughts on packaging.

A resume is your profile. The way you present yourself in it is critically important. In fact, it's so important that you might not trust yourself to write your own. Many agencies, large and small, will be happy to relieve you of that task. If you decide to go to one of them, ask to see some of their work before you contract to have your resume written.

Paradoxically, some agencies that prepare resumes don't do a very good job. So how do they stay in business? Simple. At worst, many people who use them don't know what a resume ought to have in it; at best, they don't know how a resume ought to be arranged. By now, even if you know nothing else about resumes, you at least know that the bottom line belongs up front. In clear, concise, and specific terms—immediately below a heading that contains your name, address, telephone number, and e-mail address, if you have one—your resume should tell anyone who reads it what it is you want. And it should say something about you as well. To do that clearly, concisely, and specifically, you need to come to terms with the position at issue, what that position will require of you, and what you can bring to it.

Suppose, on finding out that a particular high school has a job vacancy for a math teacher, you decide to go after it. To promote your candidacy, you attempt to come up with a new bottom line, a first cut at which might look something like this:

> **Objective:** To secure a position as a high school mathematics teacher.

That is, after all, what you want to do. Fair enough. But the initial impression made by that entry is not particularly engaging. You can begin to change it by getting answers to a couple of obvious questions: Where is the school located? How large is it? The position announcement may not say, but it will more than likely tell you the name of the school. If you have the name, what's to stop you from calling the school and finding out as much about it as you can? After you've done that, you can go back to the drawing board (the computer where you have saved the first version of your resume) and revise your bottom line:

---

[1] David G. Henderson's *Job Search: Marketing Your Military Experience,* 3rd ed. (Mechanicsburg, PA: Stackpole, 1999) is a good one for military personnel.

> **Objective:** To secure a position as a mathematics teacher in a small, rural high school.

The qualification provided by "small" and "rural" focuses your objective. In its revised form, it now targets a particular job. It also lets the folks doing the hiring know that you would not find the prospect of working at a little school in the country unattractive. That additional information conveys, however indirectly, your particular interest in working at this particular school.

The revised statement does not, though, convey as much about you as it could. While you are finding out about the school's size and location, you might also find out something about its demography. What kinds of students does it take? Do many of them go to college? Do many pursue vocational tracks? Does the school promote advanced placement? The answers to such questions should give you what you need to communicate a lot of important information about yourself in a few words. Revised a second time to highlight your teaching competencies, the entry now reads:

> **Objective:** To secure a position as a teacher of business mathematics, trigonometry, and calculus at a small, rural high school.

The people looking at your resume can tell at once that you are capable of teaching a full range of courses, and that you want to exercise that capability in their little rural school. And that first resume entry could communicate still more information without collapsing under its own weight. For instance, if you had experience as a varsity runner in college, a principal with only a modest budget to support the school's sports program might find an entry of this sort especially arresting:

> **Objective:** To secure a position as a teacher of business mathematics, trigonometry, and calculus at a small, rural high school with part-time coaching opportunities.

When it comes to looking for jobs, there are no guarantees. There are a lot of good people looking for a chance. But chances seldom fall into the laps of those who haven't done something to create them. What you do with that first entry of your resume, and the way that you structure the other entries to support the first, may well determine whether you get the chance you want.

Think about it for a minute. When do you need a resume anyway? Usually when you're leaving one job and looking for another. If the job you're leaving happens to be the military, you have a built-in progression of X number of years. And if you're proud of what you've done, you want to talk about each one of them. There's nothing wrong with that. How you talk about them, though, can be a little tricky.

Part of the human condition is our tendency to try to work up to a kind of crescendo of information. It's the same tendency chapter 5 takes up—the desire to build suspense. Our first impulse is to use the you-ain't-seen-nothin'-yet approach with resumes. That approach tells the person reading the resume that you are poorly organized and rigid in your thinking.

Preparing a resume that way will do the same thing for your appearance that dressing backwards will do. Suppose, on dressing to go out, you begin by putting on a dark business suit. Next come the shoes and a shirt. Then you pull on your socks and underwear. No question about it, you'd be fully dressed. But you'd look bad. Why have the business suit if you're not going to let it show? Put it out where people can see it. So, too, with a resume.

By the way, that metaphorical suit may not be the best-looking thing in your closet. But if your object is to look your best, pull out the best and rank the rest behind it. In other words, your best entry on a resume may not be the last thing that happened in year 29, but rather in year 26. Fine. If you find yourself having to go all the way back to year 3 or 4, writing a resume is the least of your worries.

One final point on resumes: Translate military job titles and positions into terms that make sense in the context you intend to show your resume. In other words, if you have been a fighter pilot, battalion commander, radar mechanic, operations sergeant, or submarine captain, and now find yourself looking for work of a markedly different sort, you must explain what you did in terms that correlate to management, finance, training, planning, and precise technical skills. Do not expect a marketing firm to invite you for an interview because you commanded eight hundred soldiers in sustained ground combat operations against a heavily fortified enemy, or because you maintained in combat-ready conditions 120 fighting aircraft.

That entries of that sort often fail to result in interviews does not mean that the hiring company does not hold your military accomplishments in high regard. More likely, it means that the company you want to work for is not engaged in ground combat operations or concerned with large numbers of fighting vehicles. If that company hires people, though, it might be very interested to know that you could offer extensive experience in human resources, team building, and motivational psychology. And if it happens to be a firm that pays attention to operational efficiency, your design and implementation of a system of maintenance that kept $X million in equipment and $Y million in vehicles fully operational for Z months will probably receive something more than a ho-hum.

Resumes all come down to this familiar theme: *Know your audience, know yourself, and package your product accordingly.*

SOCIAL CORRESPONDENCE

In and out of the military you should regard social correspondence as a general format. When your requirement for social correspondence is formal, you might want to consult one of the many etiquette books in print. The conventions of formal social correspondence are important, not just in terms of format, but timing too. If you don't have a pretty good grasp of this sort of thing, you need to do some homework.

If you do have confidence in your knowledge of social formats and conventions, there's no reason why you should communicate within them in any but the most effective way. People are no less happy to have a thank-you note they can understand than they are an understandable decision paper. Organize your social correspondence as efficiently as possible. At the same time, recognize that a thank-you note and a decision paper are not the same thing.

Informal correspondence can and should be handled in the same way. Unless you happen to write to people who love drawn-out convolutions of one sort or another, keep the Spartan model pretty close at hand. There's no shame in writing notes and letters that your family and friends can understand easily and quickly. Understanding and enjoyment are not mutually exclusive.

11

Argument

The fourth chapter of this book deals with substance. In doing so, it necessarily flirts with the subject of this chapter. That the flirtation does not move on to consummation in chapter 4 is a matter of context rather than the distinction between persuasion and argument. Let me explain. In operational contexts, military writers are duty bound to present their case as clearly, concisely, and sparely as the subject matter will permit.

To argue is to make a case. The evidence offered in a given case must be (1) relevant and (2) sufficient. Analysis of the evidence must be (1) thorough and (2) logically sound. The extent to which an argument succeeds is directly linked not only to (1) evidence and (2) the analysis of it, but also to (3) the skill, patience, and completeness with which both are presented. For many military writers, presentation is the least interesting and therefore the hardest requirement of argument.

When you have provided enough *substance* (evidence) and enough *analysis* (explanation) to *compel* recognition that such-and-such condition exists or, when the goal is *persuasion, to move someone to act in a given way* with a degree of confidence, you will have done your duty. Your reward for that may not always be thanks—it may not even be acknowledgment. So be it. The line of work you're in is the "service" after all.

Still, if your presentation is solid, respectful of the reader's time, and responsive to operational contexts, you will not suffer, no matter how unwelcome the news you deliver or how unpleasant the decision it demands.

But what if you're not in an operational assignment and instead find yourself in an academic or policy environment, for example? You can, of course, expect to write there as well. Writing in these kinds of assignments is considerably different than writing in operational assignments. The odds are very good that what you write in an academic or policy environment will be longer and require a lot more detail. People reading your work will be more able to take the time to go over what you say and how you say it. In an academic context, neither your readers nor you will likely share a common operational landscape. They will be less willing (or able) to fill in gaps left by the unarticulated facts or concepts to which you and a reader operating in the same setting would readily stipulate.

An argument's effectiveness depends on accuracy of information, correct computation and application of data, and timely delivery of your conclusion.

METHODOLOGY OF ARGUMENT
Whether one follows Aristotle, Cicero, Horace, Longinus, or any number of their latter-day disciples, the form and structure of an argument is, and has remained, more or less standard. Early in the presentation you must state, clearly and obviously, your *thesis,* which is the conclusion of an argument. If that sounds a lot like another enjoinder to put the bottom line up front, that's because it is. Few things will put you at odds with people reading your argument faster than making them search high and low for its thesis. Here's the first rule, then: *Put the thesis where it can be seen early and clearly.* Even in slower-paced environments, people become annoyed when your omissions translate into an abuse of their time, resources, and good will.

Earlier I referred to dialectical reasoning, the process in which thesis and antithesis square off to produce a synthesis. The root of all three words, "thesis," means "proposition," which itself means "the position you are for." Where does that position come from? From you. It is the conclusion *you* have come to in consequence of *your* (1) detailed research, (2) analysis of internal and external evidence, (3) consideration of the quantity and quality of both, (4) application of inductive and deductive reasoning, and (5) evaluation of opposing points of view. Whether you intend your argument to take the form of a treatise, monograph, essay, research paper, explication, military staff study, or article for a professional journal, the process you need to go through to generate a thesis is essentially the same.

Research
Writing in an environment receptive to argument, you may have more control over subject matter than you would in an operational setting. When you do, be sure you pick subjects you are interested in. Paradoxically, an interesting subject can be more difficult to deal with than one you would approach with indifference or disdain. Hence you will want to avoid overly emotional attachment to the topic, as this could prejudice—and discredit—

your analysis. Once you begin your research in earnest, you will discover in short order whether you are falling victim to your interest in the subject. How long it takes to make that discovery is a function of the scope of the project and the time you have available to complete it.

If the requirement is to produce an essay of 2,000 words, and you have two weeks between assignment and submission, you need to be writing a first draft by the beginning of the second week. What should you do if you find yourself knee deep in books, notes, and Internet offprints but without a clue as to the next step? Walk away from the project for a couple of hours, then go back and reread chapter 5 of this book. Using the organizational method modeled there, you should be able to see where you have too much, too little, and irrelevant material. Cull, add, and chop as you must to assemble a workable body of material to support the project.

The process I am talking about here has a name: *restriction,* or in military terms, "economy of force." Two thousand words do not give you much wiggle room. If you discover that you cannot possibly do justice to your subject in only 2,000 words, you need to restrict it. Make it brief enough to fit the form. Don't try to deal with an entire campaign, but rather with a force—and better still, with a single commander in that force during one phase or a portion of a phase. You get the idea. Adapt the amoeboid process from chapter 5 to your subject and do it graphically if necessary.

Conversely, if you find that you cannot come up with 2,000 words on a dare, use the same graphic methodology to show you where you need to focus your efforts. The object of the exercise, once you have restricted the subject to fit the given form, is to *ensure that your research has produced the evidence you need to make and support a case.* This is your second rule.

Analysis of Evidence

Analyze your evidence by looking at how it relates to your subject directly and indirectly, explicitly and implicitly. What I am talking about now is *analysis,* which amounts, on one level, to little more than a sorting process and, on another, to hard-nosed *evaluation.* How do your primary sources stack up against your secondary sources? Do they relate directly and explicitly to your topic, or does their relationship depend more upon circumstance and analogy? How many of each kind of source do you have? What value do you place on them? Which seem more reliable? All those questions are central to your analysis, but the one addressing reliability has particular importance.

Quantity and Quality of Evidence

Reliability is a litmus test for decisions on the quality of evidence. Think about this or that bit of evidence in the same way you would think about a parachute. Before I jump wearing this parachute, I would like to know what kind it is, when it was made, whether it is compatible with others I have used, and who rigged it. Based on the answers I get to those questions, I can make a judgment as to the parachute's reliability, and if I conclude it's reliable, I'll jump with it. That sort of action indicates a significant degree of confidence. Standing in the door with that parachute on, I still don't know that I'm going to be all right after I leave the aircraft, but I have taken the *internal* evidence as far as I can take it. Quite simply, there is no more.

At this point, *external* evidence becomes important. Two examples come to mind. First, all the others aboard are wearing the same parachute. One supposes (but without surveying individuals, who can know?) that each has gone through a process of parachute evaluation. Some of them have already left the aircraft and seem to be proceeding safely down under inflated canopies, though they are not yet on the ground. Second, there are my own religious beliefs. For me, they may become the most compelling evidence of all when my turn to jump comes.

Were I to argue formally for using the parachute, I would incorporate all of the internal evidence to support my thesis, and I would buttress my argument with one piece of external evidence: its apparently successful use by all who are in the process of jumping with it. The external evidence tied to my own beliefs, however important to me as an individual, has no utility in my argument. In sorting through the available evidence, qualitative judgments of that sort are critical. Don't be reluctant to make them.

Applying Inductive and Deductive Reasoning

Consciously or otherwise, you will use both inductive and deductive reasoning as you analyze your evidence. The questions I raised in the example of the parachute are *inductive* in that they move from specific pieces to a larger generalization. Induction does that for us. As children, we toddle past a hot stove, touch it, burn our hand, cry, and get over it in time. Maybe we repeat the exercise once more at a later date. A few slow learners play it out a third or fourth time. Eventually, we all reach the same generalization: A hot stove will burn my hand. We got to that by looking at a few specific instances.

In the case of the parachute, I got answers to the specific questions I asked. Those answers allowed me to generalize: This parachute is safe. Left with that alone, would I have been willing to jump with it? Fortunately, I didn't need to make that call without the reinforcement provided by *deduc-*

tive reasoning. That kind of reasoning allows me to take a generalization and use it as a basis for a very particular decision. I came to my second generalization by looking at particular evidence, in this instance the people in front of me on the aircraft and in the air below. Here's the generalization: *Persons who wear this parachute are persons whose parachutes open.* From that generalization, I move inward: *I am a person who wears this parachute.* The very encouraging conclusion I reach is this: *I am a person whose parachute will open.* Using both induction and deduction, I managed to conduct what proves a satisfactory evaluation of the evidence I had gathered. The result of that evaluation has me exiting the aircraft along with everyone else. The intent here is not to bog down in induction and deduction—trust me, you use both regularly or you wouldn't be able to survive professionally—but rather to identify another rule of argument: *Evaluate the available internal and external evidence for its quantity, quality, and reliability.*

Evaluating Opposing Points of View

What I haven't taken up yet are the opposing points of view. In the hypothetical case of the parachute, let me offer two that are obvious. The first belongs to my mother. She sees the use of any parachute for any reason as profoundly unnatural and morally dubious. Another argument, a little less visceral than Mom's, argues for the sky diver model that makes the jumper look like Batman and land like a feather. The first point of view is easily set aside on the basis of the numerous logical fallacies that are its underpinnings; the second, because the alternative it proposes is both expensive and incompatible with a tactical environment. Dealing with contrary points of view in that way causes them to drop out of the equation, which, in itself, strengthens my argument—indeed, any argument. Depending on the form your argument takes, you may or may not write explicitly about other points of view, but in formulating it, you must consider them. The rule? *Identify views contrary to yours to determine the extent to which the available evidence supports them.*

Everything I have said since urging you to state your thesis clearly and concisely early in a written argument pertains to a process that goes on inside your head. Although the example of the parachute is a silly one, the to-jump-or-not-to-jump question illustrates an internal intellectual process that has a good deal of satisfaction associated with it. In an earlier chapter I said that your job as a writer is to sketch for your reader the intellectual process you went through to get to your conclusion. Fail to do that very thing in a written argument and your entire argument will fail.

The devilish part of it all is that the delight in the process is not in writing about it after the fact, but actually going through it. Tough. It's a problem, but the problem is yours, because your readers will refuse categorically to make it theirs. They can't put themselves behind your eyes or inside your head. You must do that for them, and if you approach it the right way, you can enjoy yourself while you're doing it. You can't expect people to believe what you say unless you give them a reason to believe it, and the most obvious way to do that is to show them how your head works. For most people, that's the hardest part of the process.

Perhaps you should think of recounting your evidential analysis, which is exactly what I did in the example of the parachute, as a chance for you to show off blamelessly. It may be drudgery to you, but for your reader it's essential.

Avoiding the Boredom of Argument

The problem many people have with argument is boredom. They get fired up doing the research, have a fine time pulling their evidence together, and enjoy turning it over in their heads or chatting about it with a friend over a cup of coffee. Most folks enjoy the intellectual exercise of solving the problem. Having solved it, they want to move on to a new subject. You may feel the same way.

Stop right there.

If you think for a minute that the up-front statement of a clear, concise thesis that you believe in passionately because you know where it came from is anything more than an opening bid, you're in real trouble. The thesis statement isn't the game, but rather the ante. The game consists of a slow walk-through of the material evidence that has (1) specific detail, and (2) explanatory discussion, which you must produce to make your thesis stick when you reiterate it at the conclusion of the piece. You *do* need to reiterate it at the conclusion. Reiteration, by the way, should not be slavish repetition. By way of disengaging from this discussion, I'll offer one more rule: *Tell your reader what your evidence is, why it matters, and how it supports your thesis.*

I have not addressed methods of research or conventions of documentation, both of which are critically important. Beyond saying that you have an obligation to see to both, I will not address them further. Those topics are beyond the scope of this book. For what it is worth, though, I will say one thing about each. Concerning research, the Internet is a useful resource. It's fast, colorful, engaging, seemingly limitless—and filled with error and misinformation, as well as correct data and facts. As the old mapmakers used to inscribe on uncharted seas, "There be dragons here." Watch it! Concerning

documentation, give credit where credit is due. There be dragons here, too—
big ones.

SUMMARY

What is presented in the earlier chapters of this book informs this one as
well. Context notwithstanding, you need to support what you say with specific, concrete examples. And you need to explain them in terms of the point
you want to make. Argument, fundamentally, is the same exercise dealt with
in the majority of this book, if a bit overblown in comparison. It is a venera-
ble pattern of organization, and it will serve you well if you scrupulously
follow the few rules introduced above and repeated here:

1. Put your thesis where it can be seen early and clearly.
2. Ensure that your research has produced the evidence you need to
   make and support a case.
3. Evaluate the available internal and external evidence for its quantity,
   quality, and reliability.
4. Identify views contrary to yours to determine the extent to which the
   available evidence supports them.
5. Tell your reader what your evidence is, why it matters, and how it
   supports your thesis.

When you've done all that, edit your draft with care before making a
final copy. Toward that end, some of the suggestions in the next chapter may
be of use.

12

Editing Techniques

Few things are more frustrating than having something you've written returned with instructions to rewrite it. Where do you begin? If the person sending it back has given you no concrete suggestions for the repairs you are to make, you have a real problem.

Likewise, few things are more frustrating than reading something and knowing that it needs to be fixed, but not knowing why. That situation is particularly painful if the reader and writer happen to be the same person.

Criticizing unsatisfactory writing is easy, but criticizing it constructively is another matter. To give constructive criticism to yourself or any other writer, you must translate the visceral response—This is junk! I hate it!—into terms the writer can act on. The way you do that is by becoming an editor.

The few editorial techniques this chapter deals with won't land you a job in publishing or journalism. Learn to use them, though, and they will make you a more constructive reader and a more effective writer.

EDITING FOR CLARITY
Virtually everyone who talks about writing makes the point that it must be clear and concise. But what good does that sort of dictum do for the writer who struggles to put three sentences together? Not much.

Some years ago several reading specialists adopted a system of word and sentence counting to help them select the right texts for the right age groups. The system involves counting words and sentences and multiplying by 0.4. That factor translates the density of words and sentences into a reading age. Though by no means absolute, this formula did allow teachers to select books with more than a little hope that their students could read them.

Different versions of this formula have been called the fog factor, density gauge, and clarity index. Whatever you call it, it's a valuable tool that you can use to measure, in quantifiable terms, whether a piece of writing is clear and concise.

This formula quantifies two things: sentence length and long words. To determine the average sentence length of a given piece of writing, count a sample of about 150 to 250 words (certainly no more than 250). By the way, whether you count LTC Cougat or FM 6-40 as one or two words doesn't make any difference. Your figures should be reasonably accurate, but mathematical precision is not the issue here. The formula is a tool, not an end in itself.

After recording the number of words in your sample, go back and count the number of sentence units. Notice that I said sentence units, not sentences. Identify sentence units by looking at punctuation. Any group of words preceded by a period, question mark, exclamation point, semicolon, colon, or dash is a sentence unit. So is any sentence contained within parentheses.

Next, take the number of sentence units and divide it into the number of words. That division gives you the average sentence length of the sample. Throughout this book, I have said that your sentences should be about fifteen words long. If the average sentence in a writing sample has fewer than fifteen words, great. If it has more, you have an explanation as to why the writing is not concise: The sentences are too long.

Now you can go back and look at long words. For the purposes of this formula, a long word has three or more syllables. If determining syllabification is easy for you, then finding long words will be a snap. If it isn't, try this: Rest your chin heavily on the heel of your hand, and then say the word slowly. The number of times your chin moves is the number of syllables in the word.

Go through the sample and count the number of long words. Record it, and divide it by the total number of words in the sample. If that percentage is under 15, fine; if it's over, the constructive criticism is obvious. The writing isn't clear: There are too many long words.

You might be curious as to why fifteen words per sentence and 15 percent long words are the limits. Added, those numbers equal 30. Multiply that figure by 0.4 to get 12—the number of years of education a reader must have to understand the sample in one fast reading.

A couple of points. By striving to write on a twelfth-grade level, you are not insulting your readers. Even if they all have Oxford doctorates, they'll appreciate being able to get through your stuff quickly and on to other things. Many journalists and publishers have long recognized the need to offer their readers material written on an eighth-grade level. That doesn't mean they think their readers have eighth-grade brains; it means they know that if they don't make what they print clear and concise, their general readers will lose interest and stop reading.

From time to time you might surprise yourself by applying this formula to different things you read. Some that you thought were quite sophisticated may well turn out to demand no more than a tenth-grade education for a reader to understand them in one fast reading. Others that you would expect to be very simple will turn out to be pretty tough going. Consider this extract from the edition of FM 100-1 in use when the first edition of this writing guide appeared:

> As a derivative of the political aim, the strategic military objective of a nation at war must be to apply whatever degree of force is necessary to allow attainment of the political purpose or aim for which the war is being fought. When the political end desired is the total defeat of the adversary, then the strategic military objective will most likely be the defeat of the enemy's armed forces and the destruction of his will to resist. It is essential, however, that the political purpose be clearly defined and attainable by the considered application of the various elements of the nation's power. Not until the political purpose has been determined and defined by the President and the Congress can strategic and tactical objectives be clearly identified and developed. Once developed, the strategic objectives must constantly be subjected to rigorous analysis and review to insure that they continue to reflect accurately not only the ultimate political end desired but also any political constraints imposed on the application of military force.

That passage is the first substantive paragraph of a section of the manual dealing with the principles of war. Look at this breakdown:

Total words	171
Number of sentence units	5
Average sentence length	34 words

Right away we can criticize this passage because its sentences are too long. To continue:

Number of long words	42
Total words	171
Percentage of long words	25%

We don't have to look very hard for another piece of constructive criticism to go with the first. The passage has too many long words.

If you had trouble getting through it in a hurry, this will show you why:

Average sentence length	34
Percentage of long words	+ 25
Total	59
Conversion factor	× 0.4
Required education level	23.6

Someone with a couple of years of postdoctoral study might get through that paragraph quickly and understand it. Most readers, though, must read it pretty slowly.

What's intriguing about that particular piece is its origin. A military writer wrote it for use in a military context. A military agency supervised its editing and publication. The concept is great. Unfortunately, audience does not seem to have figured in the equation. As a writer, you know you must produce clear, concise writing. As an editor, you now have one concrete way to tell if you (and others) have produced it.

Whether others have put this system in practice is difficult to prove, but I can report some heartening evidence of improvement. Consider the summary that concludes the second chapter of FM 1, which superseded FM 100-1 on 14 June 2001:

> The Army has always been a learning institution and, because of this, it is an innovative one as well. We continuously assess changing technology, strategic and operational environments, national strategic objectives, and new threats and threat capabilities. In response to changing conditions, The [*sic*] Army determines new strategic requirements, develops operational concepts to fulfill them, and identifies the essential capabilities necessary to employ land forces as part of the joint team. Thus, strategic requirements and innovative operational concepts drive changes in Army capabilities. New operational concepts demand new equipment and materiel solutions; organizational changes to employ these capabilities; and changes in doctrine, training, and leader and Soldier development. These imperatives are interconnected, and constantly evolving; this cycle is a continuous process. In every period of change, we must carefully balance The Army imperatives. Allowing one to advance too rapidly or lag behind the others could unhinge the force. Thus, as the pace and scope of change increases, we must not only adapt, but also alter the way The Army changes. Taking full advantage of the rapid pace of development will allow The Army to

retain the ability to achieve sustained full spectrum land force dominance in the future.

Though a bit intimidating at first blush, the passage is a real improvement over the first. Here's the breakdown:

Total words	197
Number of sentence units	13
Average sentence length	15 words

Fifteen words is an upper limit, but the piece's reduced density is noteworthy. Long words are still a problem:

Number of long words	46
Total words	197
Percentage of long words	23%

Because they are, the chances that most folks will get through the passage in a single rapid reading are not good.

Average sentence length	15
Percentage of long words	+ 23
Total	38
Conversion factor	× 0.4
Required education level	15.2

Someone with a college education might manage on a single rapid reading, but that's optimistic. Others will probably need a little more than a quick once-over to take it in.

In the interest of fairness, we must recognize that neither this passage nor the manual containing it is an operational document any more than this book is. The richness and historical weight of the subject matter and the purpose of this particular manual enforce slower handling intentionally. But even when we write things that might properly be read more slowly, there is merit in paying attention to sentence length and word density.

EDITING FOR CORRECTNESS

Grammar, usage, and mechanics (though I am not a big fan of capitalizing articles along with the nouns they introduce, e.g., The Army; see Part II) were not problems in the last two examples. That won't always be the case, of course. Often you must deal with usage before you can tackle clarity. When you do edit usage, focus first on the role of the editor: to ensure that the writing getting by you can be understood in a single fast reading.

One thing that will make that possible is the absence of gross grammatical errors. Chapter 7 covers this in detail. Simply keep in mind that spelling, sentence structure, and subject-verb agreement must be correct. If the writing you edit has problems on that level, help the writer solve them. Then pass the document on. Don't tie it up just to win a relatively unimportant victory or, worse yet, just because you can.

That means you have to know the capabilities of the writers whose work you read. In the area of correctness, treat the bad ones and the good ones the same. Read their work for gross errors. Bad writers won't be able to do much more than correct the ones you point out to them. Good writers don't want you messing with their stuff if there's nothing seriously wrong with it. Focus on the basics with these two groups, and leave everything else alone.

The so-so writers are another story. This group can respond to and learn from your guidance on more than just gross errors. Misplaced modifiers, dangling participles, pronoun references, uses of commas—all these things and more you can productively address with this group. And you should, until they themselves become good writers. Then leave them alone as well.

Clearly you should do all you can to improve the writing you are responsible for, whether you are author or editor. Keep this in mind: Worry second about flawless usage. *Your first worry is effective communication.* If you get art in the process, that's fine. If you don't, it wasn't your job to get art anyway.

USING A HIGHLIGHTER

How you mark what you edit makes a big difference to the people who write it. If you return their work with cramped marginal notes, arrows, additions, deletions, crossovers, etc., you aren't helping much. First of all, those marks may be unfamiliar. Often they're hard to read, and they obscure the original writing. And if you make them in volume, you take too much of the rewriting burden on yourself.

You can overcome most of these problems by using a highlighter. Don't use it to write with; rather, use it as a signal. Advise the people whose writing you read that you will mark errors in usage and lapses in style with a highlighter. If you see a mistake, simply run the highlighter through it. That's all you need to do and all you should do.

An obvious advantage of a highlighter is its bright color. It directs the writer's eyes to the exact spot needing correction or change without obscuring it. Sometimes you must write explanatory comments or instructions to supplement a highlighted passage. When you do, use a pencil. That way, you can always change your mind without making a mess on the document.

To repeat: Tell the people whose writing you edit that you use a highlighter. Tell them why you use it and what you expect them to do in response to it. Once you've done that, you'll be pleased to learn that a whole lot of additional comment simply isn't necessary. Editing with a highlighter means less work for you. The person doing the rewriting is the writer, not the editor. And that's the way it should be.

EDITING FOR STYLE

One of the hardest things editors must do is let their own pet peeves pass unchanged when they don't impede effective communication. Face it: Sometimes changing "however" to "moreover" is simply an exercise in power. And that's nonsense. Changing "and" to "but" is another matter, though. Be sure you know the difference. Use your power when effectiveness is at stake; when the choice is simply a matter of personal taste, let the writer alone. It's hard to do, but do it anyway.

Some stylistic matters that you shouldn't let pass have to do with voice, vocabulary, and jargon. As chapter 6 urges, keep writing in the active voice whenever possible. Inhibit the practice of creating verbs from nouns (verbalization) and nouns from verbs (nominalization). Keep jargon at a minimum. In a word, do everything you can to shorten and streamline the writing in front of you.

You don't have to be a wizard to change the style of much of the stuff you read. Merely by using the highlighter you can work wonders. Look at this extract from a Department of Defense regulation on supply management:

> Within DOD, shelf-life items will be identified on storage locator records by shelf-life codes set forth in appendix A and applicable shelf-life condition codes set forth in appendix B. In addition, items will be identified in storage location records within condition codes, by either the earliest date of manufacture/cure/assembly/pack, by the earliest date of expiration (type I), or the earliest inspection/test date (type II). Whenever a discrepancy between the storage records and the records of the ICP with respect to shelf-life code or condition codes becomes apparent at the storage level, action will be initiated at the storage level to reconcile all records. This will be accomplished by preparation and processing of change of condition codes (DIC DAC), DD Forms 1225, Storage Quality Control Reports, and related documents, to the appro-

priate ICP. Additionally, controls will be established to assure shelf-life material is inspected and reclassified into appropriate condition codes based on instructions provided by the ICP.

Notice that the highlighter has done nothing more than draw attention to forms of the verb "to be." If, in pencil, the editor added this note—Rewrite without forms of the verb "to be"—the passage would be easy enough for the writer to revise.

By the way, there are other things in this unrevised sample you might want to highlight. Look at it again:

Within DOD, shelf-life items will be identified on storage locator records by shelf-life codes set forth in appendix A and applicable shelf-life condition codes set forth in appendix B. In addition, items will be identified in storage location records within condition codes, by either the earliest date of manufacture/cure/assembly/pack, by the earliest date of expiration (type I), or the earliest inspection/test date (type II). Whenever a discrepancy between the storage records and the records of the ICP with respect to shelf-life code or condition codes becomes apparent at the storage level, action will be initiated at the storage level to reconcile all records. This will be accomplished by preparation and processing of change of condition codes (DIC DAC), DD Forms 1225, Storage Quality Control Reports, and related documents, to the appropriate ICP. Additionally, controls will be established to assure shelf-life material is inspected and reclassified into appropriate condition codes based on instructions provided by the ICP.

In this second version, the highlighter directs the writer's attention to the poor use of verbs, a doubtful pronoun reference, and two annoying instances of connecting words with diagonal strokes. All these things are stylistic; if the piece were in the active voice, the shrewd editor might let them all pass in the interest of time. However, since it has to be rewritten to get it out of the passive voice anyway, it ought to be cleaned up to look something like this:

Identify shelf-life items by shelf-life codes in appendices A and B. Identify items in storage location records within condition codes by their earliest dates of manufacture, expiration (type I), or inspection (type II). Storage facilities must reconcile discrepancies between records and shelf-life or condition codes. Do that by submitting completed DD Forms 1225, Storage Quality Reports, etc., to the concerned ICPs. Based on instructions from those ICPs, inspect and reclassify shelf-life material to ensure its proper control.

Responding to the highlighter, the writer can recast the sample in the active voice, shorten the passage considerably, and make it more accessible to the reader. When the editor gets the revision, if he thinks something of substance has fallen out, he simply needs to put it back—but put it back in the style of the revision.

As you become more sophisticated in editing for style, you will be able to work faster and with more confidence. For starters, though, follow these guidelines:

1. Use a highlighter to do your marking.
2. Use a pencil to write any instructions you have for the writer.
3. Highlight forms of the verb "to be," nominalizations, verbalizations, and jargon.
4. Never make a writer change what is already effective writing just because you can.
5. Remember: Rapid reading and understanding are the goals of your editing—not art.

EDITING FOR ORGANIZATION

There's one fundamental point to be made here, and it can be made quickly. If the first significant entry in a given document isn't the bottom line, the document must be rewritten. It's as simple as that.

One other consideration: If headings would help the reader but there are none, send the document back to the writer for headings.

REWRITING

In a military context, the main function of editors is to save time. Whose time? First, there is the time of the readers who need to act on the documents editors release. Clear, concise, correct, organized writing saves readers' time. That's why editors need to insist on it.

Next, editors must save their own time. One document is a drop in the proverbial bucket. That means that editors don't have a lot of time to spend rewriting the stuff they read. And even if they had the time, using it that way would be a mistake. What do writers learn by having their work rewritten by someone else? Little.

Editors must keep the burden of rewriting where it belongs: with the writers. The techniques this chapter suggests will help editors do precisely that—and in constructive ways.

PART II

A Checklist of Grammar, Usage, and Mechanics

In the process of trying to finish various writing assignments, many people turn anxiously to others for help with grammar, usage, and mechanics. "Hey, Joyce, is it all right to begin a sentence with a number, or do I have to spell out 612?" and "Should I say 'less marines' or 'fewer marines,' Major Bloggs?" are familiar kinds of questions. And there's nothing wrong with asking them, so long as the people you ask know what they're talking about.

When they don't know, or when you're too embarrassed to ask those who do, this chapter is where you ought to turn. Though not in any sense a comprehensive guide to English, what follows does have the answers to most of the questions a military writer is apt to ask.

a, an. Whether you use the indefinite article *a* or *an* depends on sound. If the word following the article has a vowel sound, you must use *an;* if it has a consonant sound, then use *a.* Spelling is not an issue in this case. The sailor wears *a* uniform even though *uniform* begins with a vowel. By the same token, we refer to *a* howitzer and *a* historian (the practice of using *an* with words beginning with the letter *h* followed by a vowel is virtually extinct). There are exceptions: The exchange opens *an* hour later today, for instance. But the basis for such exceptions is sound. Likewise, we talk about *an* aviator because of the vowel sound of the word *aviator.*

abbreviations. In formal writing, abbreviations should not be used as a rule. That does not mean the exclusion of standard abbreviations; rather, it means a letter from a flag officer to a command group should wish people a Merry Christmas (not Xmas), mention the new chaplain (not chap.), cite a book (not bk.), and spell out words such as *please* and *without* as opposed to abbreviating them as *pls* and *w/o.* Those kinds of abbreviations make perfect sense in an interoffice note or on a routing slip, however.

On the other hand, certain standard abbreviations do have their place in formal military writing. For example, CPT (Capt.), TM, AFM, and CSM are all examples of standard abbreviations that properly might be used in formal military prose. How to use them is the issue.

> **Wrong.**   I saw CPT Wilbur Smith and another CPT.
>
> **Right.**   I saw CPT Wilbur Smith and another captain.
>
> **Wrong.**   It was in TM 21-6 or another TM.

Right.   It was in TM 21-6 or another technical manual.

There's nothing mysterious in any of that. In a formal context outside the military you would follow the same guidelines.

Wrong.   I met Dr. Harold Gar and another Dr.

Right.   I met Dr. Harold Gar and another doctor.

Pay attention to punctuation of abbreviations. Most governmental abbreviations do not use a period; indeed, it is wrong to use one with them. Other abbreviations do require punctuation. What you need to know is which do. One obvious tip-off is that governmental abbreviations tend to be in capital letters or uppercase type: CDR, PV2, and so on.

Other standard abbreviations require punctuation. Some examples worth remembering:

Dr.	Rev.	Jr.	e.g.	B.C.	St.
Mr.	Ms.	Fr.	etc.	A.M.	Mrs.
et al.	*c.* or *ca.*	Sr.	i.e.	A.D.	P.M.

Governments in general and the military in particular make far greater use of abbreviations than other organizations. That practice, for all its advantages, has obvious drawbacks that you need to be aware of when you write. Common sense should tell you two things about using abbreviations: First, in formal writing don't embarrass yourself or the person who must sign your work; second, in informal writing don't abbreviate to the extent that what you say can't be understood.

abridged clauses. In these constructions, the subject and a form of the verb *to be* get left out of a dependent clause. Using them from time to time will save you some words. When all you have is the space of a single sheet, that can be important. Some examples:

Unabridged.   When he was first assigned, he dreaded the prospect.

Abridged.   When first assigned, he dreaded the prospect.

Unabridged.   After he had been manning the bridge for two hours, he was relieved.

> **Abridged.**   After manning the bridge for two hours, he was relieved.
>
> **Unabridged.**   While I was at Fort Sill, I studied gunnery.
>
> **Abridged.**   While at Fort Sill, I studied gunnery.

absolute phrases. These phrases save words because they modify whole sentences rather than just parts of sentences. Use them when they seem appropriate, but be sure you use them correctly and without creating dangling modifiers or comma splices (see entries for more on these two errors). A lot might be said about absolute phrases, but for our purposes it's sufficient to say they are created by getting rid of a form of the verb *to be*. Compare these examples:

> **Original.**   The anchor having been lowered, the ship stopped drifting.
>
> **Absolute phrase.**   The anchor lowered, the ship stopped drifting.
>
> **Original.**   The barrage having been silenced, movement again resumed.
>
> **Absolute phrase.**   The barrage silenced, movement again resumed.

accept, except. These two words are frequently confused. To *accept* something is to receive something, to admit something, or to answer affirmatively:

> She eagerly accepted her new command.
>
> You must accept responsibility if this ambush fails.
>
> I accept your recommendation.

To *except* something means to leave it out or exclude it:

> Let's except sergeants major from the test.
>
> All marines in the company except Sanders are good swimmers.

active voice. A verb is in the *active voice* if it defines an action or state of being for the subject of the verb; in other words, if the subject is doing the acting rather than being acted upon. Some examples:

> The mess sergeant cooks. [active voice, present tense]

> The mess sergeant cooked. [active voice, past tense]

> The mess sergeant is cooking. [active voice, present tense with present participle]

Here's another definition of active voice: a verb not made up of a past participle with a form of the verb *to be*. Note, however, that you can use a form of the verb *to be* and still write in the active voice. Look back at that last example. Or look at these:

> He *is* the new gunnery sergeant.

> I *am* Captain Sawyer.

adapt, adopt. These two words are frequently confused. They do not mean the same thing. To *adapt* is to adjust or modify:

> He *adapted* the generator to run on less fuel.

It can also mean to become adjusted to:

> Good soldiers will *adapt* to fighting in arctic conditions.

To *adopt* means to take on:

> C Troop *adopted* the puppy as a mascot.

or to follow by choice:

> Our wing *adopted* the new beret with pride.

adjectival clauses. There are many kinds of clauses. This particular kind functions as an adjective. That is, an adjectival clause will modify (tell us something more about) a noun or a pronoun. Here are a couple of examples:

Captain Zimmer, *who was my rater for two years,* has just retired.

Where's the moonlight *that was supposed to make this night march easy?*

Use them when you need to give more detail than the noun or pronoun gives by itself.

adjectives. Writers use adjectives to modify nouns—to tell their readers more about those nouns than they would know without them. For instance:

Corporal Andersen is a marine.

Corporal Andersen is a *good* marine.

Corporal Andersen is an *old* marine.

As those examples show, adjectives precede the things they modify when you use simple word order. Most of the time that's the order you should use. Occasionally, though, it may suit your purpose to use a more complicated word order. Against that chance, here are some examples showing adjectives set apart from what they modify:

Their uniforms, *torn* and *soiled,* smelled of cordite.

Our march, *only six hours long,* will begin after breakfast.

When you break away from simple word order, be sure you have a good reason. In the case of the two examples, the reason was a matter of emphasis. The first is the sort of sentence you might use in writing a unit citation; the second, to shore up failing morale.

Before you fill your writing with adjectives, look carefully to see if you're really searching for better nouns. Instead of *withered old woman* use *crone;* instead of *old soldiers* go with *veterans;* instead of *spiritual leader* try *chaplain.* Cutting down on adjectives by picking the right noun in the first place is another way of shortening what you write.

Sometimes you will have to put several adjectives together in a series. When you do, separate them with commas in this way:

Her clean, white, and highly starched uniform was torn.

Lieutenant Washington found the rusty, broken shovels hidden in the supply room.

Don't get carried away with the commas, though. Use them as a tool to help your readers understand what they're reading. Here's an example of getting carried away:

Lieutenant Washington found six, rusty, broken shovels.

This is more like it:

Lieutenant Washington found six rusty, broken shovels.

adverbial clauses. These dependent clauses work the same way adverbs do: They modify verbs, adverbs, and adjectives. Their function is to give more information about the things they modify. If you don't need such information to make your point, though, don't use them. Some examples:

Ever since she received her orders, Private Asher has been ready to leave.

Commander Freebish runs this office *as if he had three times the staff.*

After the patrol left cover, Specialist Thomas was injured.

adverbs. Adverbs modify verbs, adverbs, and adjectives. In a sentence they can crop up almost any place and still make pretty good sense. For instance:

Private Winston *confidently* fired his rifle.

Confidently, Private Winston fired his rifle.

Private Winston fired his rifle *confidently.*

Since they can move around on you, adverbs are not always so easy to find in a sentence. One thing will help you a little: Most adverbs end in -ly. Most do, but not all.

Those that don't end that way can be a little confusing at first look. *Now, then, here, there,* and *when* are all adverbs. They come to us today out of Old English; hence they don't have the *-ly* ending. But they're easy enough to recognize and deal with. The ones that may be a little trickier for you are those that look the same way they look when they're adjectives. Here's a partial list:

bad	even	long	straight
better	fast	much	tight
close	funny	right	well
deep	high	sharp	wrong

Those, and many other words like them, function as both adverbs and adjectives. For example:

Airman Peters and I had a *close* [adjective] call. Next time we'll know not to sit so *close* [adverb] to the edge.

This is a *deep* [adjective] channel. In patrolling it we can run silent and *deep* [adverb].

And some of those same words will have a second identity as adverbs when they take on an *-ly* ending. For instance:

badly	deeply	tightly
closely	sharply	wrongly

Be careful! They may not have the same meaning in the new configuration that they have without the *-ly* ending.

The commander felt *badly* about the results of the inspection. He also felt *bad* because he had buttermilk and sardines for breakfast.

Most adverbs end with *-ly,* but many, as you have seen, don't. So how do you know if you're working with an adverb? There's nothing to it, really. First, find the verb; second, find the word you think may be an adverb. Look at that word and see if it tells you anything about the verb (or, by extension, another adverb or an adjective). If it's an adverb it will tell you where, when, how, how much, or why. To illustrate:

Outdoors [where], the unit performs *well* [how].

The troops had *fully* [how much] cleared the underbrush once *before* [when] lunch.

Then they ate *hungrily* [why and how].

Use adverbs sparingly. If you have already made your point in other ways, you don't need to beat it to death with adverbs. Instead of writing

The rotten tent leaked *everywhere.*

just write:

The rotten tent leaked.

The adverb *everywhere* gives you another word without giving you much more meaning in exchange. By definition, rotten tents leak. What more is there to say? You can drop *everywhere* without loss.

adverse, averse. Do not confuse these words. Adverse means hostile or unfavorable:

Adverse seas delayed our landing for two days.

Major Sommers has an *adverse* fitness report in his file.

Averse means opposed or reluctant:

The crew chief is *averse* to the new maintenance schedule.

Sergeant Wiggons seems *averse* to taking charge of things.

Neither word, by the way, is particularly good for military writing. If you're bent on using them, though, use them the right way.

affect, effect. These two words will get you into trouble if you can't keep them separate. Each is a noun and each is a verb. Don't think of them that way, though. Treat affect as a verb that means to influence. Think of effect as a noun that means a result. Compare:

Smoking cigarettes will *affect* your stamina and health.

Lung disease is often an *effect* of smoking cigarettes.

Many military writers use *effect* as a verb meaning to cause or bring about. For instance:

The new captain *effected* many changes on the destroyer.

Given the confusing nature of these two words, you're better off sticking with *effect* as a noun and saying instead:

The new captain made many changes on the destroyer.

Besides, even if you know the difference in how these two words are used, you have no guarantee that your reader will. When you can, avoid using *effect* as a verb.

agreement. Chapter 7 deals with this subject in detail. The point to stress here is that subjects and verbs must agree in number. Singular subjects need singular verbs; plural subjects need plural verbs. Examples:

Wrong.   Six *trucks is* missing spare tires.

Right.   Six *trucks are* missing spare tires.

Wrong.   The *chief want* this scope repaired.

Right.   The *chief wants* this scope repaired.

Chapter 7 touches on the matter of pronoun-antecedent agreement, but not in any real detail. Here's the rule: *Pronouns and their antecedents must agree in gender, person, and number.* Some illustrations:

Wrong.   Everybody needs to check their shot records.

Right.   *Everybody* needs to check *his* or *her* shot records.

Wrong.   *Each* of you *are* volunteers, right?

Right.   *Each* of you *is* a volunteer, right?

Wrong.   *Anyone* who wants a pass must see *their* squad leader.

Right.   *Anyone* who wants a pass must see *his* or *her* squad leader.

Everybody, each, anyone, somebody, another, anybody, and words like them are singular. They take singular pronouns. Pronoun-antecedent agreement mistakes with such words, even if the result of an effort to use nonsexist language, make the writer look bad. Don't make them.

Longer sentences where antecedent and pronoun are fairly far apart may cause you some problems. Two solutions:

1. Write shorter sentences.
2. Pay attention to what you are saying.

For example:

Wrong.   The *difficulties* the landing party regularly has in the early stages of establishing its beachheads, particularly if enemy resistance is strong, are *that* dealing with close air support.

Right.   The *difficulties* the landing party regularly has in the early stages of establishing its beachheads, particularly if enemy resistance is strong, are *those* dealing with close air support.

Pronoun-antecedent agreement is not hard to master. Just pay attention to the gender, person, and number of what you're talking about. A few more examples:

With land in sight, the *members* of the crew are anxious to take *their* shore leaves.

Colonel Morrisot, despite expectations to the contrary, will fire *his* best round of the tournament today.

Though *he* knows *she* rarely says much in public, *Airman Kelley* still needed to tell *Sergeant Watson* why *she* did not report *her* findings to *him* earlier.

a lot. There is no such word as "alot." A *lot* means much or many. Don't make the ignorant mistake of spelling it as one word.

all ready, already. All ready means that everyone is prepared:

> My troops are *all ready* to cross the phase line, but I have my doubts about Company C.

Already is an adverb meaning by a specified time:

> By nightfall I want your squad *already* dug in.

all right. No matter how many other ways you see it spelled, all right is the only correct spelling of this phrase meaning satisfactory, OK, unharmed, right, doubtless, and yes.

also. This adverb means too, as well as, and plus. Though it isn't incorrect to begin sentences with also, it's generally a bad idea because it makes your writing seem weakly organized. For instance:

> The first midshipman tightened the lines. Also he cleated them.

Better to write:

> The first midshipman tightened and cleated the lines.

although, though. These words mean the same thing. Although is somewhat more formal than though. You may use them interchangeably except in a case like this:

> **Wrong.** The lead track was late getting in convoy position, *although.*

> **Right.** The lead track was late getting in convoy position, *though.*

alumna, alumnus. These words from Latin mean the same thing: former student or graduate. *Alumna* refers to one woman; *alumnae* to two or more women. *Alumnus* refers to one man; *alumni* to two or more men. When referring to a mixed group, use *alumni.*

amend, emend. *Amend* means to improve, add to, or change. *Emend* means to edit. Examples:

New intelligence estimates force us to *amend* the plan.

Too many writing errors force us to *emend* the plan.

among, between. Use *among* when talking about more than two of a given category. For instance:

Private Bardolph was *among* six soldiers who pulled their reserve parachutes.

Use *between* when referring to two:

Sergeant Bushy and Lieutenant Bagot spread the map out *between* them.

amount, number. When referring to mass, use *amount:*

Our five tons seem to be burning a large *amount* of diesel.

Use *number* when referring to things that can be counted:

Private Bolingbroke looked over a *number* of gas pods before finding two that weren't defective.

and. This word's function is to connect. It has three main uses:

1. To join independent clauses
2. To link parallel constructions
3. To connect the last two elements in a series

When used to connect independent clauses, *and* must be preceded by a comma:

The two landing craft arrived on station late, *and* the company failed to secure its objective.

The new gasket is in position at last, *and* now the tanker can proceed without losing any more oil pressure.

Any two grammatical units of the same sort—parallel constructions such as two adjectives, say, or two nouns—are joined by *and.* To illustrate:

The sergeant major sent for *and* talked to Sergeant Francis and Private Drake.

The first soldier seemed quiet *and* nervous; the second was obviously anxious *and* very pale.

Unless you have very good stylistic reasons for not doing it, connect the last two elements of a series with *and*. Some examples:

Captain Hereford arrived at the office, cleared his desk, called for the first sergeant, *and* reached for the inbox.

The rotor blades are unpainted, warped, *and* dented.

You can also use *and* to begin sentences if you want to connect thoughts from sentence to sentence. This practice is effective only if it is not over-worked. Be careful.

and/or. Do not use this construction in an attempt to be all things to all people. You wouldn't say "Good morning, ladies and/or gentlemen." Don't write it either.

antecedent. The antecedent is the thing a pronoun refers to. When you write, try to put antecedents *before* the pronouns that ultimately represent them. This is an example of that kind of sentence order:

The *marine* saw *his rifle* and picked *it* up.

You can, of course, have an antecedent follow the pronoun that refers to it. Consider this example:

We didn't find *him* until the smoke cleared to reveal *Captain Falstaff* lying there.

If you decide to write that way, though, be sure the relationship between those two elements will be understood by your reader.

any. This word can be an adjective, an adverb, or a pronoun. As an adjective it means no matter which or some. Examples:

The chief said *any* bunk would suit the new mate.

Does the new guard have *any* special orders?

As an adverb, *any* means to a degree or extent; or it means at all. Examples:

Although he has been "on quarters" for three days, Major Chillblain still doesn't feel *any* better.

After practicing the maneuver every day for two weeks, the new drivers won't get *any* better at it than they are now.

As a pronoun, *any* means anyone or any part. Examples:

If you need rangers, *any* from the 75th Regiment will do.

We have no JP-4 at this site. Do you have *any* to spare?

apostrophes. The primary use of apostrophes is to show possession. Here are a few simple rules for their use:

1. Form the singular possessive by adding an apostrophe followed by an *s:*

the pilot's log, the driver's wrench, the rigger's lines

2. Form the plural possessive by adding an apostrophe *after* the final *s,* unless there is none (as in men):

the ladies' meeting, the doctors' operations, the men's room

3. Form plurals of words ending in *s* by adding an apostrophe and another *s* unless it sounds bad:

Sergeant Ross's platoon, Colonel Watts's brigade, Rogers' Rangers

Apostrophes are also used in contractions to show where a letter has been omitted. For the word to be spelled correctly, either the missing letter or the apostrophe replacing it must be present.

> **Wrong.**   dont, donot, wont, willnot, cant, can not
>
> **Right.**   don't, do not, won't, will not, can't, cannot

appositive. An appositive is a word (usually a noun) or group of words used with another noun to give information that the noun itself does not. Usually, appositives are set off by commas. Some examples:

> Private Hotspur, *the best driver in the company,* is on orders to Japan.
>
> Captain Odysseus, *a weak swimmer,* is nevertheless a fine sailor.

The only time appositives are not set off by commas is when they are what we call restrictive: when they limit the noun they are related to and could not be removed without jeopardizing the meaning of the sentence. For instance:

> The woman *who gave the order* is my commander.

The appositive in that example restricts the sentence by identifying the woman being talked about. The woman is my commander. Well, which woman is that? The woman *who gave the order.*

as, like. *As* is a conjunction; *like* is a preposition. When using these words to set up comparisons, keep straight as to what each one is. For most of the writing you do in the military, you can get away with using them interchangeably. Of the two, *as* is more formal. But when using *as* starts to sound stuffy to you, replace it with *like*. In fact, you ought to make *like* your standing first choice. Some examples:

> She marches *like* a soldier.
>
> She marches *as* a soldier should march.
>
> Captain Hendon screamed *like* a mashed cat.
>
> Captain Hendon screamed *as* a mashed cat might scream.

Incidentally, it should be obvious to you that *as* forces you to use more words than *like*. Keep that in mind.

auxiliary verbs. These verbs will make your writing longer. Sometimes you can't avoid using them, though. Some of the more common ones are:

be	may	should
can	might	will
do	must	would

When used with other verbs, these verbs form different moods, tenses, and voices. We also use them to ask questions (*Did* the motor officer arrive in time?); contradict (The motor officer *has* not arrived yet); and emphasize (The motor officer *did* arrive in time).

Without auxiliary verbs, those sentences could not exist. On that basis, we might view them as necessary. Sometimes, though, they may not be. "I eat" and "I am eating" mean the same thing. Unless you have some stylistic or tonal consideration for writing "I *am* eating" instead of "I eat," you should opt for the shorter version.

awhile, a while. *While* is a noun. When used as the object of a preposition (in *a while* or after *a while,* for instance) it should be spelled as two words. *Awhile* is an adverb. As such, it is used and spelled as one word. For example:

Airman Percy will be out of the hangar *awhile* this afternoon.

bad, badly. Perhaps the best way to keep these words straight is to think of *bad* mainly as an adjective and *badly* as an adverb. *Bad* can also be an adverb:

Captain Marcus felt *bad,* so he went home.

If you need a more formal tone, get rid of *bad* and replace it with a better adverb:

Captain Marcus felt ill, so he went home.

be. This verb is one we cannot do without in our writing. It is the most commonly used verb in the language. That owes, in part, to our willingness to use it to death. Valuable as it is, *be* is also a weak verb that makes what we write longer and less effective than it would be without it.

This verb has eight different forms:

am	are	be	been
being	is	was	were

You cannot write in the passive voice without using one of those eight forms of the verb. If you can do it no other way, ensure that you write in the active voice by making a conscious effort to drop them from your vocabulary, at least when you get tempted to use them with other verbs.

Except for excessive use of the passive voice, military writers don't have too much trouble with this verb. Sometimes, though, finding the right case for the first- and third-person pronouns causes some confusion. What's the right response to this question: "Who goes there?" Do you say "It's me" or "It is I"? And how do you answer this one: "Who fired that last round?" Is the right response "It was she" or "It was her"?

Most of the time, whether you use the subjective case (I, he, she, we, they) or the objective case (me, him, her, us, them) is a function of how formal you want to be. Notice I said *most* of the time. Sometimes, to use the objective case is simply gross. There are no easy solutions to this problem, but most of the time you can stay out of trouble by following this rule: *Informally, use pronouns in the objective case; formally, use pronouns in the subjective case.*

because. Use this subordinating conjunction to give the reason for whatever statement you make in the main clause. For example:

> *Because* he had pulled targets all morning, Private Luxon needed a break.

> Private Luxon needed a break, *because* he had pulled targets all morning.

Either way the reader knows why Private Luxon needed a break.

One final point: Never use *because* to write "my explanation is because" or "one reason is because."

beside, besides. One way to keep these two words straight is to think of *beside* as a preposition and *besides* mainly as an adverb (*besides* is also a preposition). *Beside* means next to or near. The adverb *besides* means in addition; the preposition *besides* means in addition to. Some examples:

> The captain set his tent up *beside* the fire direction center.

He set up two other tents *besides* [adverb].

And *besides* [preposition] setting up the tents, he dug a trench.

between, among. When referring to two of a particular class, use *between;* use *among* when referring to three or more. Examples:

Lieutenant Redcrosse sat *between* Lieutenant Duessa and Captain Fradubio.

Specialist Una knew she was *among* friends when she recognized six other squad members sitting in the rear of the plane.

between you and me. When you use this construction, the pronoun must be in the objective case (see examples under the entry for *be*). "Between you and I" is a gross error and "Between she and I" even worse. Both errors, and their variants, grow out of the overly conscientious effort to appear correct. A good alternative to appearing correct is to be correct. Learn the rule.

black, white. These two words represent two different colors. As it turns out, those colors happen to be used to designate two distinct racial groups: Negroes and Caucasians. Notice that *Negro* and *Caucasian* require a capital letter. The adjectives *black* and *white,* when they stand for Negro and Caucasian, usually do not. Times change. *Negro* is now used only in anthropological studies and in names of organizations. *Black* (capitalized, noun) is becoming the accepted name for members of the Negro race.

brackets. Unless you are editing quoted material, you probably won't have occasion to use brackets in military writing. In this section I have used brackets to set off material that really isn't part of the text at hand. I have done that in the interest of clarity. That's the same motive for using brackets in quoted material too. If you need to add a word or two to make a quoted passage fit in with your text, use the brackets to let your reader know precisely where. An example:

"Captain Malbecco sent for his forward observer [Lieutenant Bumpo] well ahead of schedule. When the observer arrived [2100 hours on 5 May], the unit had already deployed."

In a case like that, use brackets instead of parentheses. Parentheses do not tell the reader that the material contained in them is an addition to the original text. Brackets do. But do not use brackets unless you are inserting something into a quotation. To insert something in your own writing, use parentheses rather than brackets.

but. In terms of what it does and the way you need to punctuate it, *but* works pretty much the same way as *and:* It serves as a coordinating conjunction to connect units of equal grammatical weight.

But obviously will connect two independent clauses; you will often use it to connect statements in opposition. It will also connect parallel constructions—two adverbs, say, or two adjectives. And you can use it, though in moderation, to begin a sentence. Finally, you can use it as a preposition meaning except. Here are some examples illustrating its uses:

> Private Boswell has been in boot camp for only three days, *but* he has already shown that he has what it takes to be a fine marine.

> This soldier frequently suffers from skin rashes, *but* a visit to Dr. Johnson ought to help him with that problem.

> Sergeant MacHeath landed heavily *but* safely.

> Say what you want to about Colonel Peacham: He's hard *but* fair.

> We looked for signs of enemy activity and found none *but* a spent shell casing.

> Everyone in the stick is here *but* Lockit.

c., ca. These are abbreviations for the Latin word *circa.* They stand for *approximately* or *about* and are normally used with dates. Except in the most remarkable circumstances, they have no place in military writing.

can, may. For military writers these words have basically two functions: to ask permission and to express a possibility. In the subjunctive mood, their forms are *could* and *might,* which also happen to be the past-tense forms of *can* and *may.* Beyond a certain point, don't worry about any of that.

What you need to know is this: *Can (could)* has to do with ability; *may (might),* with permission. When expressing possibility you would be technically correct to use either. If all that seems overly complicated, make it easy on yourself. Follow these rules:

1. When talking about possibilities, use *may*.

   If he's late to formation again, the platoon sergeant *may* get angry.

   Sergeant Schmidt *may* go back to Germany if he gets the chance.

   Come what *may,* as long as we have ammunition we stay here.

2. When you want to talk in terms of ability, use *can*.

   Specialist Rosencrantz *can* run a chart better than anyone else in his battalion.

   When it comes to taking charge, Captain Grabbit *can* teach us all a few tricks.

   If they possibly *can,* the three tankers will land, refuel, and be airborne by 1500.

3. When asking permission to do something, use *may*.

   I want to submit this requisition quickly, but before I do anything more on it, *may* I talk with your S-4?

   Sir, *may* I make a comment?

   I hate to turn down this request, but Corporal Homer *may* not have eight six-day leaves in succession.

Now, a few examples of *could* and *might:*

   Before I undertake this mission, *might* [permission] the command not spend a little more time explaining its purpose?

   Private Alving *could* [ability] be a first-rate soldier, but he isn't.

   Sergeant Hudson *could* [possibility] help you if he were here, but he's away from garrison conducting reconnaissance.

can't hardly. Colloquial or not, *can't hardly* is wrong. *Hardly* means scarcely or probably not. Using it with *can't* creates a double negative. The proper phrase is *can hardly.*

can't help but. This idiom is generally accepted. Sometimes, though, you may wind up writing for someone who prefers you to use the nonidiomatic *can't but.* Both mean the same thing. The second configuration is technically the more correct of the two. Use it if you must; otherwise, go with the more common *can't help but.*

capital letters. Military writers tend to get a little carried away when using capital letters. That tendency probably reflects an attempt to add emphasis to a particular passage, but capital letters may not be the best way to do that. One exception: After a colon, you may want to begin what follows with a capital letter (as I have done here) to make it more emphatic. There's nothing wrong with that if you don't wear it out.

Most of the time, you won't have any trouble using capitals if you follow these conventions:

1. Begin sentences with a capital letter.
2. Begin quoted sentences with a capital letter. If you break a quotation in midsentence, do not use a capital letter when you resume it:

> "This perimeter defense plan," Colonel Jones continued, "is not adequate."

3. Use capital letters with proper names and with titles that are part of such names. Examples:

Donald Romero	Conn Barracks	Marine Corps Marathon
Chaplain Donald Romero	Company C	Thanksgiving
Chaplain Romero	Negro	Third Division Band
Hudson River	Army	Fulda Gap
Army Regulation 635-212	Monday	TM 22-5
Gore Boulevard	15 April	Battle of the Bulge

4. Use capital letters for high office when the person holding the office is mentioned by name. Examples:

President George Washington	Captain John Paul Jones
Queen Elizabeth II	

The Hon. George C. Marshall, Secretary of State
General Dwight D. Eisenhower, Supreme Commander

What about titles without proper names, such as secretary of defense, president of the United States, commodore, chairman of the Joint Chiefs of Staff? If such positions are important in the context you're writing in, use capitals. If they aren't, don't.

5. Religious denominations and deities require capitals. Examples:

Catholic	Baptist	Mohammed	Messiah	Islamic
Episcopal	Holy Spirit	Protestant	Savior	God
Jesus	Prophet	Jewish	Virgin	Allah

6. Capitalize nouns, pronouns, verbs, adjectives, adverbs, and prepositions of more than five letters in the titles of books, speeches, articles, plays, essays, etc. You must also capitalize the first and last words of titles, and the first word after a colon. A few examples:

The Eagle Has Landed
Two Years Before the Mast
Our Defense Today: A Reconsideration

case. Case shows the relationship of a noun (or pronoun) with another part of a sentence. Nouns don't cause many problems for writers, but pronouns seem to be a bit more difficult. Most commonly, that difficulty occurs when a pronoun follows a linking verb such as *to be* (the most common linking verb).

For more discussion of pronouns and linking verbs, see the entry on *be* above. The issue is not so much a matter of being right or wrong (though in the strictest sense it probably is), but rather of being formal or informal. That distinction turns on whether you follow the linking verb with the nominative (subjective) case or the accusative (objective) case. To illustrate:

Formal.   It was I. It is he.

Informal.   It was me. It is him.

Another area of confusion is the distinction between *who* (nominative) and *whom* (accusative). This time, the accusative case is the more formal.

Formal.   With *whom* were you assigned to stand guard.

Informal.   *Who* were you assigned to stand guard with.

Formal.   Captain Bartin is the officer to *whom* you were speaking.

Informal.   Captain Bartin is the officer you were speaking to.

There are right and wrong ways to use *who* and *whom*. For example:

Wrong.   He is the one *whom* gave us permission [i.e., him gave us permission].

Right.   He is the one *who* gave us permission [i.e., he gave us permission].

The genitive (possessive) case has several functions. The one you should be most concerned with has to do with showing possession. "The *rifle of the soldier* [genitive] is missing" means the same thing as "The *soldier's rifle* [possessive] is missing." Showing possession with an *apostrophe s* will save you the words *of the* that the genitive case uses.

Elliptical constructions—those that drop words because the meanings of such words can be inferred from another construction—using *than* or *as* will sometimes trip you up. Remember, when you use *than* or *as* you are making a comparison; remember, too, that you want it to be grammatical.

Some examples:

Wrong.   The captain always gets to work earlier *than* me [i.e., earlier than me do].

Right.   The captain always gets to work earlier *than* I [i.e., earlier than I do].

Wrong.   Sergeant Morse knows the codes as well as *them* [i.e., as well as them know the codes].

Right.   Sergeant Morse knows the codes as well *as* they [i.e., as well as they know the codes].

censor, censure. To *censor* is to remove objectionable material; to *censure* is to blame or criticize harshly. Compare:

> Captain Bowdler, afraid of *censure* from headquarters, painstakingly *censored* the controversial report.

cite, site. Do not mistake these words. To *cite* is to quote, refer to, commend, or call to court. A *site* is a place where something was, is, or will be. To illustrate:

> Headquarters will *cite* Lieutenant Crusoe for his ability to survive so well on such an unfriendly *site.*

clauses. A clause is a grammatical unit with a subject and a predicate. Some clauses are independent, which means they are also sentences. Example:

> Sergeant Swift called on the new supply sergeant.

Other clauses are dependent. Dependent clauses also happen to be subordinate clauses; that is, they must be joined to another part of a sentence with a subordinating conjunction. Subordinate clauses are not complete sentences unto themselves. Some examples:

> that it was time to empty the bilge

> who saw little change in the weather

> when Specialist Quince reported for duty

Subordinate clauses are named for the job they do in a sentence. Those that act as subjects or objects are called noun clauses. Examples:

> **Subject.**   *That it was time to pump out the bilge* was obvious to the engineer.

> **Object.**   The engineer knew *that it was time to pump out the bilge.*

Adjective clauses work the same way adjectives do. For example:

> **Adjective.**   The pilot *who saw little change in the weather* took off at noon.

And adverb clauses function in this way:

Adverb.   The exhausted RTO was delighted *when his replacement reported for duty.*

collective nouns. Nouns whose singular form names several people, deeds, or things are called collective nouns. Here are some of the common ones:

Air Force	corps	number
audience	court	platoon
battery	fleet	section
committee	group	unit

In its singular form, you can treat a collective noun as either singular or plural and still be right. Once you decide which you want it to be, though, you must not change your mind. To illustrate:

The *platoon* is in *its* night position, and *it* has all listening posts in place.

The *platoon* are in *their* night positions, and *they* have all listening posts in place.

Both examples are correct. A British writer might have written the second and an American the first. The second version looks at the platoon as individuals; the first treats it as a unit. When you write for an American audience, you would do well to follow the American convention.

colon. There are many uses for colons. Military writers need to be aware of four: separating a series or a list from the rest of a sentence; qualifying the idea or statement that comes immediately before the colon; introducing quoted material; and emphasizing material that would, without the emphasis, come after a semicolon.

1. You may separate a series or list from the rest of a sentence as I have done in the preceding paragraph. You may also present a list as a list—that is, in columnar order—depending on the stylistic effect you want to produce. An example of that kind of list appears at the end of chapter 1.

2. Use a colon to qualify, expand, or explain the idea that comes just before the colon. For example:

We need to improve sanitation in the barracks: Start flushing the toilets.

> Rigging involves a lot of work: repairing torn chutes, untangling lines
> and risers, and refitting broken hooks.
>
> *The Navy in the Second World War: An Illustrated History*

3. As a rule, if you quote less than five lines, you should introduce that material with a comma. Sometimes, for emphasis, you might want to introduce a quotation with a colon, even if the quotation is no more than a phrase. If you decide to do that sort of thing, don't beat it to death.

4. For emphasis' sake, you may want to use a colon where you would ordinarily use a conjunction or a semicolon. For instance:

> Major Wright was able to land successfully, because he was able to
> compensate for a loss of power in the left engine.
>
> Major Wright was able to land successfully; he was able to compensate
> for a loss of power in the left engine.
>
> Major Wright was able to land successfully: He was able to compen-
> sate for a loss of power in the left engine.

All three sentences say the same thing, but the way they say it is not the same. Tonally, the third is the most intense. That's a function of the colon. Like a double reverse, it's a gambit that probably won't work twice in a row. Keep that in mind.

comma. This punctuation mark has a lot of rules governing its use. You don't need to know them all. In fact, they're all subordinate to this one: *Use commas in such a way as to promote quick reading and clear understanding of what you write.* That doesn't mean you should ignore all the other rules; it just means you should subordinate other considerations to getting the job done as quickly, clearly, and painlessly as you can.

Unless you have a pretty compelling reason to do otherwise, abide by these guidelines:

1. Use commas to separate independent clauses joined by a coordinating conjunction. Examples:

> The supply warrant was on TDY for three weeks, but his shop did not
> fall apart during his absence.

Cadet Watson could not decipher the code, so he decided to take it to Sergeant Major Holmes.

2. Use commas to set off dependent clauses or long phrases that introduce the main clause of a sentence. Examples:

Falling several times after starting, Airman Forbes still finished the confidence course in record time.

With no regrets, Captain Nemo turned over command of the carrier to Captain Douglass.

Staring intently, Corporal Barnes continued to look through the badly damaged starlight scope.

3. Use commas to set off nonrestrictive modifiers. Examples:

The battalion's most effective writer, Captain Huxley was the logical choice to replace the departing adjutant.

Captain Huxley, the battalion's most effective writer, was the logical choice to replace the departing adjutant.

4. Separate items in a series with commas. Go ahead and put a comma between the next-to-last and last items of a series. If those items are punctuated internally, you must separate them with semicolons. Examples:

Sergeant Raphael assigned three soldiers to dig a trench, four more to clear brush, and two others to put in trip flares.

Every marine needs identification tags, a watch, eight magazines of ammunition, and a clean rifle.

Admiral Gruenther's children were born in Richmond, Virginia; Aberdeen, Scotland; Washington, D.C.; and Naples, Italy.

5. Parenthetical expressions—however, moreover, of course, then, etc.—must be set off by commas. Examples:

However, Major Palestrina was a superb drill instructor.

Major Palestrina, however, was a superb drill instructor.

Major Palestrina was, however, a superb drill instructor.

6. Separate two or more adjectives or adverbs that modify the same word in the same way with commas. For instance:

The unit just received six new, inexperienced soldiers.

Notice that *six* and *new* do not need to be separated by a comma. Why? *Six* tells how many soldiers and *new* tells what kind: The two adjectives don't modify soldiers in the same way. *New* and *inexperienced* do modify soldiers in the same way; both tell what kind of soldiers, and they need a comma between them.

comma splice. A comma splice occurs when you try to join two independent clauses with a comma instead of a coordinating conjunction, semicolon, or colon. It is a particularly gross error. Pay special attention to avoid making it. Some examples:

Wrong.	Commodore Post and Admiral Watts served together for years, they respect each other greatly.
Right.	Commodore Post and Admiral Watts served together for years, and they respect each other greatly.
Right.	Commodore Post and Admiral Watts served together for years; they respect each other greatly.
Right.	Commodore Post and Admiral Watts served together for years: They respect each other greatly.

comparison of modifiers. By using a process called comparison, we express adjectives and adverbs in one of three degrees: absolute, comparative, and superlative. Form these degrees by adding *-er* (comparative) or *-est* (superlative) to the basic modifier (absolute). Or form them by preceding the basic modifier (absolute) with *more* (comparative) or *most* (superlative). A few irregular formations—e.g., good, better, best—you simply must memorize. Some examples:

	Absolute	**Comparative**	**Superlative**
Adjectives	tired	tireder	tiredest
	tired	more tired	most tired
	martial	more martial	most martial
	good	better	best
Adverbs	often	oftener	oftenest
	often	more often	most often
	vigorously	more vigorously	most vigorously

Notice that in some cases (e.g., *tired*) comparatives and superlatives can be formed either way; in others (e.g., *vigorously*), you must use *more* and *most*.

Use the comparative when showing the degree of difference between two people, places, or things and the superlative with three or more. For instance:

Captain Ramar is *better* in the jungle than Captain Gallant.

Of the four divers, Seaman Bell seems *best* for this mission.

Caution: Be sure that when you use comparatives you really are comparing. Illustrations:

Wrong.   Corporal Pearson's score on the PT test was even worse than Private Wilson.

Right.   Corporal Pearson's score on the PT test was even worse than that of Private Wilson. [wordy]

Right.   Corporal Pearson's score on the PT test was even worse than Private Wilson's. [less wordy]

Right.   Corporal Pearson scored worse on the PT test than Private Wilson. [least wordy]

complement, compliment. Confusing these words will mark you as a boob in the eyes of those who know that a *complement* is something that completes or adds to the whole and a *compliment* is an expression of praise or act of civility. These words exist as both nouns and verbs. Examples:

> Your squad *complemented* this operation and contributed to its success. You all deserve to be *complimented*.

> Colonel Flynn reported with his *complement* of troops, saluted the senior commander, and offered his *compliments*.

complements. The noun or adjective that follows a linking verb is called a *complement*. Its function is to complete; that is, to add meaning where a linking verb does not tell the reader enough. Note the difference:

> **Uncomplemented.** Apprentice Mercutio received.

> **Complemented.** Apprentice Mercutio received a *lengthy chewing out* from the chief.

> **Uncomplemented.** In my judgment, the brigade's report is.

> **Complemented.** In my judgment, the brigade's report is *fine*.

complex sentences. Chapter 7 deals with this subject in some detail. Here, suffice it to say that complex sentences are made up of one independent clause and one or more clauses that can't stand alone. Examples:

> Unless the situation gets much better than it is, Sergeant Moffit will have to move his platoon to the rear.

> Chaplain Chasuble visited every man in sick bay several times a day, although many didn't know it.

compound-complex sentences. Chapter 7 deals with compound-complex sentences in some detail. As their name suggests, they are the most complicated sentences.

They consist of two or more independent clauses and at least one dependent clause. Sometimes they can be very effective. Most of the time, though, military writers should leave them alone. Why? Because following their syntax does not always promote fast reading. Here's an example:

> Because he had done a superb job on the flight line, Sergeant Brabantio received the Air Force Commendation Medal, but with typical modesty he seemed embarrassed by all the attention he was receiving; in fact, he looked like he might want to go hide in one of the nearby hangars, even though he knew that was out of the question.

compound predicate. A sentence with two or more verbs (and their modifiers) for the same subject has a compound predicate. Sometimes you can use compound predicates to shorten your writing. Compare:

> The headquarters received the requirement later than expected. However, the staff responded to it quickly. Our report, written this afternoon, went out with the mail at 1700. [3 sentences, 27 words]

> Headquarters got the requirement late but responded to it quickly. This afternoon we wrote, staffed, and mailed our report. [2 sentences, 19 words]

compound sentences. Chapter 7 treats compound sentences in some detail. They consist of two independent clauses joined together by a coordinating conjunction (e.g., *and, but,* etc.), a semicolon or colon, or a conjunctive adverb (e.g., *however, hence,* etc.). Examples:

> The modification work order is here, *but* we haven't applied it yet.

> The flu shots are rescheduled: Report to the hospital at once.

> Dinner will be in two hours; *however,* the first cook says he may be able to have it ready sooner.

compound subjects. Using two or more subjects with the same verb will produce a compound subject. Compound subjects may save you a few words in your writing. When using them, be careful that you don't make a lot of inadvertent agreement errors such as the one in this example:

> His *valor and fidelity* was unquestioned.

Valor and *fidelity,* though frequently linked together in some contexts (promotions, for instance), are still far enough apart to be thought of separately; hence, they require a plural verb.

His *valor and fidelity* were unquestioned.

A few other examples:

Battery A arrived at once. Company C arrived a few minutes later.

Battery A and Company C arrived a few minutes apart.

Sergeant Balthazar entered the orderly room. Sergeant Dogberry was with him.

Sergeants Balthazar and Dogberry entered the orderly room together.

conditional clauses. There are basically two kinds of conditional clauses: those of a real-world sort and those that are contrary to fact. The first kind describe conditions that are likely to happen; the second, those that aren't. Both kinds may be introduced by words such as *if, when, unless,* and *whether.*

To use conditional clauses correctly, you need to pay attention to verb forms. The real-world type take a simple form of the verb in the conditional clause and a simple or future form of the verb in the clause being modified. For example:

If the unit *fails* this inspection, the commander *will be relieved.*

Whether you *like* it, your guard mount *begins* in ten minutes.

When the new tanks *come* on line, *we'll have* fewer maintenance problems.

Unless we *hear* otherwise, *plan* on leaving the maneuver area before dawn.

Conditional clauses that are contrary to fact take a form of the verb in the subjunctive mood. You probably won't use this kind of conditional clause too often in military writing. But when you do, use it right. Some examples:

If I *were* you, I *would ask* for a board of review.

If reinforcements *were coming*, they *would have been* here by now.

If you *were* serious about dropping that equipment from the books, you *would have dropped* it months ago.

conjunctions. Conjunctions are of two broad types. Coordinating conjunctions join grammatical units of essentially equal weight; subordinating conjunctions introduce phrases, statements, and clauses that modify something in an independent clause.

Which conjunction you use will greatly affect the tone of what you write. Be as precise as you can be in selecting the right conjunction for what you want to communicate. These examples will illustrate what I mean:

Sergeant Phipps got ill, *and* Captain Franks could do nothing.

Sergeant Phipps got ill, *but* Captain Franks could do nothing.

Sergeant Phipps got ill, *since* Captain Franks could do nothing.

Sergeant Phipps got ill, *because* Captain Franks could do nothing.

Sergeant Phipps got ill, *when* Captain Franks could do nothing.

Sergeant Phipps got ill, *yet* Captain Franks could do nothing.

Sergeant Phipps got ill, *while* Captain Franks could do nothing.

Sergeant Phipps got ill, *whereas* Captain Franks could do nothing.

Notice how in each of those sentences the view of Captain Franks changes. In some, he is the victim; in others, the victimizer; in still others, somewhere in between.

conjunctive adverbs. Use conjunctive adverbs, preceded by a semicolon and followed by a comma, to join two independent clauses. Some of the more common conjunctive adverbs are *however, moreover, therefore, hence, furthermore, nevertheless,* and *thus.*

Be careful not to overuse conjunctive adverbs. They can make your writing more difficult to get through than it needs to be. Sometimes, though, they can be quite effective. For example:

Two destroyers had severe damage to their hulls; *nevertheless,* both managed to stay afloat.

Several of our fighters are overdue for quarterly services; *moreover,* two need extra work on their hydraulic systems.

consensus of opinion. A *consensus* is a collective sample of opinions. *Consensus of opinion* is a redundancy. Never disgrace yourself by making the too-frequent error of using that expression.

contact clauses. Contact clauses and comma splices look the same. What makes one a comma splice and the other a contact clause is a function of what the writer knows. Contact clauses belong more to narrative prose than to the sort of writing you will routinely do in the military. Examples:

Comma splice. Sit down, Private Jacobs, we've been expecting you.

Contact clause. Sit down, Private Jacobs, we've been expecting you.

The first example is regarded as a comma splice because it joins two independent clauses without a coordinating conjunction, conjunctive adverb, semicolon, or colon. Though the second example looks the same as the first, in certain contexts—narration and dialogue, for instance—the apparent error is in fact a conscious stylistic device that the writer can get away with because the two clauses are short and closely related. Having a very tolerant reader also helps.

The best advice for military writers tempted to use contact clauses: Don't.

continual, continuous. Don't confuse these words. Continual means recurring frequently; continuous means uninterrupted. For example:

The motor officer has made *continual* efforts to keep the unit's trucks on the road, but the *continuous* shortage of qualified mechanics has made his job an impossible one.

contractions. Chapter 6 gives considerable attention to contractions. They are an informal form of expression, but they sometimes have a place in formal writing. When using contractions (*wasn't, aren't,* etc.) be sure to include the apostrophe to show where a letter is missing.

coordinating conjunctions. Conjunctions that link two more or less equal grammatical units are called coordinating conjunctions. Some of the more common ones are *and, but, so, yet, for,* and *or.* When you use a coordinating conjunction, you must precede it with a comma.

correlative conjunctions. Correlative conjunctions come in pairs and should be used with units that are grammatically similar. They include *either/or, neither/nor, as/as,* and *not only/but also.* Pay particularly close attention to subject-verb agreement when you use nouns or pronouns as the subjects that you link with correlative conjunctions. Here's the rule: *The second noun (or pronoun) of the correlation determines whether you need a singular or plural verb.* Examples:

Wrong.	Neither a grenade launcher nor a machine gun are needed for this mission.
Right.	Neither a grenade launcher nor a machine gun is needed for this mission.
Wrong.	The crew chief said either a cannon or two machine guns is what he needs.
Right.	The crew chief said either a cannon or two machine guns are what he needs.
Right.	The crew chief said either two machine guns or a cannon is what he needs.

When you use *either/or* and *neither/nor* as correlating conjunctions, be sure the correlation you are setting up is legitimate in terms of its numbers. Another easy rule: *Use either/or and neither/nor only when you are dealing with two persons or ideas.* Examples:

Wrong.	Either Chief Jones, Chief Brighton, or Chief Roosevelt will get the mission.
Wrong.	Sergeant Wilson recognized that Airman Sithers must either change the batteries, find a candle, or work in the dark.

> **Right.** Either a carrier-launched air strike or a land-based artillery attack can reach the target.

Neither/nor can get you into double-negative trouble if you use this correlative conjunction carelessly. Here's an example of the kind of correlation you should avoid:

> Neither not being trained nor not having supplies is an acceptable explanation.

One final point has to do with parallelism. It goes like this: Balance the elements that you link with correlative conjunctions. Examples:

> **Wrong.** Neither train too much nor discover you have too little ammunition.

> **Right.** Neither train too much nor too little.

> **Right.** Neither carry too little ammunition nor too much.

could, might. Like *can* and *may,* these two words will give you problems if you don't get their meanings straight. *Could* is the past tense of *can* and, thus, has to do with ability; *might,* the past tense of *may,* has to do with permission or probability. See *can* and *may* for examples of correct usage.

could care less. This expression is frequently (and incorrectly) used to express the total indifference correctly expressed by *could not care less.* Neither expression has a place in military writing.

criteria. *Criteria* is the plural of *criterion.* As such, it takes a plural verb. Using *criteria* with a singular verb marks you as someone having real limitations.

> **Wrong.** The *criteria is* too severe for anyone here to meet *it.*

> **Right.** The *criteria are* too severe for anyone here to meet *them.*

dangling modifiers. Generally located at the beginning or the end of sentences, these constructions fail to modify the things they are supposed to relate to. Avoid this error by putting the modifier as close as you can to the word or words you want to modify. To illustrate:

Dangler.	Driving rapidly into the track park, the ramp got in his way.
Right.	Driving rapidly into the track park, he had to stop because of the ramp.
Better.	As he drove into the track park, the ramp got in his way.
Dangler.	Frequently jamming during firing, he could not make the rifle shoot twice in a row.
Right.	Since it frequently jammed during firing, the rifle would not shoot twice in a row.
Better.	Frequently jamming during firing, the rifle wouldn't shoot twice in a row.

dash. Though not often seen in military writing, the dash is a useful punctuation mark. Produce it on a keyboard by striking the hyphen key twice. A dash can serve you in four ways:

1. Set off a parenthetical phrase. Example:

Some of the units positioned well behind the reserve force—our two truck companies, for instance—are at half strength.

2. Emphasize what follows it. Example:

This command expects only one thing from its troops—their total dedication to the mission.

3. Qualify what has gone before it. Example:

Young Werther is a model cadet—smart, enthusiastic, capable, fit, and very eager to have more responsibility.

4. Change the direction of a passage. Example:

The pharmacist mate's skill—if we can dignify his ability in that way—leaves a lot to be desired.

demonstrative adjectives. *This, that, these,* and *those* are words that show or demonstrate. When used to modify nouns or other adjectives, they function as adjectives. For instance:

> *this* very poor soldier

> *that* sergeant

> *these* badly rusted projectiles

> *those* new recruits

demonstrative pronouns. *This, that, these,* and *those* by themselves are demonstrative pronouns. They will sometimes seduce you into making reference errors—that is, your reader will not be able to figure out what those words refer to—if you aren't especially careful.

One way to avoid such errors is to use *this* and *these* when the thing, person, or idea you are referring to comes after the pronoun. For example:

> It all comes down to *this:* We move at dawn.

In the example, the pronoun *this* refers to the information that follows it: *We move at dawn.*

On the other hand, try to use *that* and *those* when the thing, person, or idea you're referring to comes before the pronoun. Consider this example:

> We move at dawn. It all comes down to *that.*

In the second example, *that* looks back at the material that precedes it.

You won't make many reference errors with demonstrative pronouns if you follow this rule: *When the referent follows the pronoun, opt for this or these; when the referent comes before the pronoun, use that or those.*

> Pointing to several boxes of ammunition at his feet, the trainer directed, "Put your grenades with *these.*"

> Pointing to several boxes of ammunition behind him, the trainer directed, "Put your grenades with *those.*"

dependent clauses. Chapter 7 treats dependent clauses in some detail. They are clauses that have subjects and verbs but cannot stand alone as sentences. Examples:

> When the new commander arrives

> Once we get into position

direct objects. Direct objects are nouns that receive the action of transitive verbs. Examples:

> The sonar operator took four *soundings.*

> The pilot returned the *charts* to the navigator.

discreet, discrete. *Discreet* means having good judgment; *discrete* means a separate thing. To illustrate:

> Private Enobarbus was *discreet* enough not to mention Captain Antony's absence from formation.

> Calibration data are *discrete:* What applies to the base piece will not apply to the number two gun.

disinterested, uninterested. Avoid the embarrassment of confusing these words. *Disinterested* means impartial or objective; *uninterested* means indifferent. Compare:

> We get our test umpires from another division to make sure they are *disinterested* in the evaluation. Unfortunately, they often turn out to be *uninterested* in working very hard at umpiring.

dived, dove. Both *dived* and *dove* may be used as the past tense of *dive.*

division of words. When you run out of room on the right side of the paper, you must divide words that won't fit by breaking them into syllables. Show the break with a hyphen (e.g., po-si-tion, how-it-zer), and finish the word at the left margin of the next line. Here are a few easy guidelines:

1. If you aren't sure of a word's syllabification [is it ho-wit-zer or how-it-zer?], look it up.

2. Divide words with double consonants between those consonants [syl-la-ble].

3. Don't try to divide one-syllable words.

4. Don't separate only one letter from a word [bus-y, a-rouse].

double negatives. To use double negatives is to make a particularly gross error. "Don't use no double negatives" really means "Use double negatives." The correct way to state the rule is "Use no double negatives" or "Don't use double negatives."

double prepositions. In colloquial speech double prepositions crop up on a pretty regular basis. For instance:

> They would not get *off of* the radio.

> He stayed *outside of* the wire all night long.

In both examples (and thousands of others like them) the *of* is unnecessary. Save the extra word and instead write:

> They would not get *off* the radio.

> He stayed *outside* the wire all night long.

due to. This phrase is in transition. Technically, *due to* is adjectival and should not be used instead of *owing to* or *because of.* More and more writers use it that way, though. The easiest way for you to stay out of trouble with *due to* is not to begin a sentence with it. Within the sentence itself, your chances of using it correctly are pretty good.

each. This singular pronoun may cause you some problems with agreement. You can manage them, though, if you remember that *each* is always singular and simply abide by this rule of subject-verb agreement: *Singular subjects take singular verbs.* Examples:

> **Wrong.**   *Each* of the infantrymen *carry* out the mission well.

> **Right.**   *Each* of the infantrymen *carries* out the mission well.

Each also invites pronoun-antecedent errors. Chapter 7 discusses some that have recently appeared because of a general effort to avoid gender-based language. Here are a few examples:

Wrong. *Each* of the soldiers performed *their* duty well.

Right. *Each* of the soldiers performed *his* duty well.

Better. *Each* of the soldiers performed *his* or *her* duty well.

Best. All the soldiers performed their duty well.

The moral? If your solution to a grammatical problem seems likely to create a cultural one, seek a compromise that will solve both.

each other, one another. Don't contribute to the confusion that exists in the usage of these phrases. Quite simply, *each other* refers to two; *one another* to three or more. Examples:

In the darkness the *two* scouts could not see *each other.*

In the darkness the *seven* squad members could not see *one another.*

editorial we. Sometimes confused with the so-called *royal we,* the *editorial we* has the potential to annoy some military readers precisely because of that confusion. To avoid that annoyance, a lot of writers retreat to the passive voice. Don't make that mistake. The *we* you avoid by using the passive voice usually isn't an *editorial we* or a *royal we* anyway. Take a look at the discussion of personal pronouns in chapter 6.

effect, affect. An *effect* is a result; an *affect* is an influence. Think of *effect* as a noun and *affect* as a verb, and you will probably be able to avoid misusing either. Unfortunately, many military writers use *effect* as a verb meaning to bring about or cause. In doing that they unwittingly contribute to the confusion between the two words. Avoid that usage if you can. If you can't avoid it, keep your wits about you. Consider these distinctions:

Shortness of breath is one *effect* of not exercising.

Shortness of breath *affects* your combat endurance.

We're *effecting* programs to improve fitness.

e.g. This abbreviation stands for the Latin phrase *exempli gratia* and means "for example." Do not confuse it with *i.e.,* the abbreviation for the Latin phrase *id est,* meaning "that is."

either. This pronoun, like *each,* takes a singular verb. Example:

| **Wrong.** | *Either suit* the commander. |
| **Right.** | Either *suits* the commander. |

either/or, neither/nor. These correlative conjunctions will not lead you into making agreement errors if you keep in mind two things. First, *either* and *neither* are singular. Second, if one member of the compound subject that these conjunctions work with is plural, the verb must agree with the nearer subject. It's not as complicated as it sounds. Look at these examples:

Wrong.	Either Sergeant Banquo or his *men* is lost.
Right.	Either Sergeant Banquo or his *men are* lost.
Right.	Either his men or *Sergeant Banquo* is lost.

ellipsis. This punctuation made up of three spaced dots (. . .) indicates the omission of words and is usually used in quoted material. When you put an ellipsis at the end of a sentence, you need a fourth dot. Why? Ellipsis or no, you still must have a period at the end of a sentence.

else. If you use *else* to show possession with such pronouns as *anybody, everyone,* and *nobody,* you must add an *'s.* Examples:

Wrong.	They are nobody *else* goggles.
Right.	Are these someone *else's* ammunition magazines?
Right.	Is anyone *else* present for duty?

emend, amend. *Emend* and edit mean the same thing; *amend* means to change or improve. This example illustrates the distinction:

The new first sergeant needs to *amend* the company's SOP for doing paperwork. He knows it, and he has already begun to *emend* the company clerk's copy.

eminent, imminent. Military writers frequently use *imminent,* which means about to happen. If you're one of them, don't confuse it with *eminent,* which means distinguished. Here's an example pointing out the difference in the two words:

The arrival of General Cloten, that *eminent* warrior and statesman, is *imminent.*

et al. This Latin abbreviation for *et alii* means "and others." Use it only as a kind of last resort and only when referring to people. Note that this abbreviation needs a period after the word *al.* Example:

The conference included General Bruegel, Admiral Bosch, Mr. Mattsys, *et al.*

etc. This Latin abbreviation for *et cetera* means "and so on." Use it when referring to things other than people. Put a period at the end of the abbreviation. An example:

The troops had all their gear: shelter halves, pegs, shovels, ground mats, *etc.*

euphemisms. These "inoffensive" phrases take the place of direct, concrete, "offensive" words or phrases. *Police action* is a euphemism for *war; injured* for *wounded; losses* for *kills;* and so on. Use euphemisms when you must, but given a choice, come out and say whatever it is you need to say. Like other half-truths, euphemisms have a way of turning on the people who use them.

every. Do not confuse *every* with *all. Every* means *each* with no exceptions. In formal usage, *every,* like *each,* takes a singular verb. As with *each,* efforts to use *every* without introducing a gender bias invite agreement errors. Pay close attention to the way you use either word. Examples:

Wrong.   *Every* sailor will have *their* two-day liberty.

Right.	*Every* sailor will have *his or her* two-day liberty.
Better.	*All* sailors will have *their* two-day liberty.

except, accept. To exclude something is to *except* it. *Accept,* on the other hand, means to take on or receive something. Here's the difference:

> If we *except* the motor officer from accountability, who will *accept* responsibility for the missing toolboxes?

exclamation point. This punctuation mark seldom makes an appearance in military writing. Perhaps that's just as well. Usually the surprise of seeing it is enough to make your reader stop. If that's your desired effect, fine; if it isn't, stick with the period.

farther, further. Be careful not to confuse these two words. *Farther* has to do with distance; *further* with an addition. Note these distinctions:

> Both submarines traveled much *farther* than we expected them to; *further,* they covered the distance in record time.

> The forward observer traveled *farther* north than he thought he would. That miscalculation *further* delayed the battery's registration.

fewer, less. When you are comparing things that can be counted, use *fewer;* when you are comparing things that have to be measured, use *less.* Examples:

Wrong.	The platoon has *less* people than it will take to turn back an attack.
Right.	The platoon has *fewer* people than it will take to turn back an attack.
Wrong.	We need to use *fewer* ammunition than we used last year.
Right.	We need to use *less* ammunition than we used last year.

foreign words. When you use foreign words you must do two things. First, be sure that your reader will know what they mean; second, put them in italics. When writing by hand or typing, indicate italics by underlining, not with quotation marks.

former, latter. Avoid referring to *former* and *latter;* instead, use *first* and *second* or *first* and *last.*

fractions. When working with numbers as numerals, express fractions as numerals as well (e.g., 1, $1^3/_8$, 6, $^1/_2$). Otherwise, spell them out in your writing (e.g., two thirds, four fifths). Note: Do not use a hyphen to express spelled out fractions unless the fraction consists of a number that would ordinarily take a hyphen (e.g., fourteen twenty-thirds, which is to say, $^{14}/_{23}$).

fragments. Sentences must have a subject and a verb, and they must express a complete thought. A grammatical unit that fails to do these things is a fragment. Chapter 7 talks about fragments in some detail. Some examples:

Fragment.	Before Sergeant Morris arrived.
Sentence.	Sergeant Morris arrived.
Sentence.	Before Sergeant Morris arrived, Colonel Bortin had gone.
Fragment.	Depending on the situation.
Sentence.	Depending on the situation, we will either attack or reinforce.

fused sentences. Chapter 7 treats fused sentences at some length. Suffice it here to say that fused sentences are run-on sentences that connect two independent clauses without punctuation or coordination. For example:

Wrong.	We take off at dawn be ready to go.
Right.	We take off at dawn: Be ready to go.
Wrong.	The budget won't support these requisitions this quarter you'll have to resubmit them in two weeks.

Right.   The budget won't support these requisitions this quarter,
                  so you'll have to resubmit them in two weeks.

genitive case. You can show possession in two broad ways: by using *'s* or
by using the genitive case. The genitive case requires you to use the word *of,*
so it is not the most economical solution to the problem of possession. But
there are clearly times when it is superior to using *'s.* For example:

Awkward usage.   Sergeant Jackson's jeep's lights are broken.

Better usage.   The lights of Sergeant Jackson's jeep are broken.

When showing possession of two coordinate nouns—e.g., *Private
Brown and Private Greene's tent*—you put the *'s* with the second noun only.
With the genitive, that same phrase comes out: *the tent of Private Brown and
Private Green.* The form you use to show possession is generally a matter of
style. When you can choose, use the *'s.*

gerund. This verbal form may give you some difficulty. It looks exactly like
the present participle, but it happens to be a noun. Compare:

Participle.   Corporal Sykes came *running* down the tank trail.

Gerund.   *Running* does not come easily to Corporal Sykes.

The most common error writers make in using gerunds is a failure to
show possession. You can avoid this mistake by knowing whether you want
the word at issue to be a verb (participle) or a noun (gerund). Knowing that,
you can punctuate your writing properly. Examples:

Participle.   This afternoon, Private Albert is *firing* his rifle.

Gerund.   Private Albert's *firing* continues to improve.

Participle.   The battalion makes too much noise when it is *moving*
                   at night.

Gerund.   The battalion's *moving* at night makes too much noise.

One other complication: Gerunds, like the verbs they derive from, can vary in voice and tense. For example:

> *Moving, shooting,* and *communicating* [present tense, active voice] are the hallmarks of the artillery.

> *Having moved, shot,* and *communicated* [past tense, active voice] were the greatest pleasures of the old artilleryman.

> *Being recognized* [present tense, passive voice] as a first-rate map reader pleased the young lieutenant.

> *Having been recognized* [past tense, passive voice] as a first-rate map reader gave the young lieutenant perhaps a little more confidence than he should have had.

gobbledygook. This derisive term characterizes the kind of euphemistic, stilted, and essentially uncommunicative writing that comes out of so many military, bureaucratic, and governmental pens. Avoid using gobbledygook by determining what it is you need to say, and then writing it in such a way that your reader can understand it in a single rapid reading.

good, well. Keep these two modifiers straight by thinking of *good* mainly as an adjective (example 3 below). In informal usage, *good* can also be an adverb (example 1). *Well* is both an adjective (example 3) and an adverb (example 2). Compare:

> There was entirely too much work to do, so Seaman Salario did not feel *good* about the new billet.

> The drinking water is contaminated, and that may be why Seaman Salario does not feel *well.*

> Once back on his feet, Seaman Salario showed us that a *well* sailor, even under a lot of pressure, can turn out *good* work.

got, gotten. *Got* is the past tense of *get;* it is also the past participle. An alternate past participle of *get* is *gotten.* Except to emphasize possession (e.g., Sergeant Boggs hasn't *got* any more ammunition) or compelling necessity (e.g., We have *got* to take this man to the dispensary now), use either form of the past participle.

hanged, hung. Both words serve as the past tense and past participle of the verb *to hang*. Except when talking about execution by hanging, use *hung*. Examples:

> All the troops reported with their identification tags *hung* around their necks.

> Airman Foster was severely shaken, for, like the others, he had never before seen a man *hanged.*

hopefully. This adverb, which means filled with hope or in a hopeful way is one of the most grossly abused words in the language. Do not use *hopefully* when you mean to say "I hope" or "it is hoped." Examples:

Wrong.   *Hopefully,* the resupply truck will arrive soon.

Right.   I *hope* the resupply truck will arrive soon.

Right.   Private Pollyanna arrived *hopefully,* but his spirits fell
                    as soon as he saw the condition of the equipment.

hyphen. There are several ways to use hyphens. A few are particularly important to military writers.

In the division of words, a hyphen shows the reader that the balance of the divided word appears at the beginning of the next line.

You also need to use a hyphen when spelling out whole numbers up to a hundred. Forty-nine, twenty-four, and sixty-one, for instance, all take a hyphen.

Compound modifiers take a hyphen when they come before the noun they modify. A few examples:

twenty-one-gun salute	four-gun battery
big-footed soldier	eighteen-year-old recruit
self-serving decision	able-bodied seaman
wild-eyed prisoner	two-by-two column

Note: Do not hyphenate compound modifiers that include an adverb ending in *-ly*. A compound modifier that includes an adverb in another configuration does take a hyphen. Examples:

Wrong.   The *badly-wounded* sailor slept fitfully.

Right.   The *badly wounded* sailor slept fitfully.

Wrong.   The *well written* operations order made perfect sense.

Right.   The *well-written* operations order made perfect sense.

I. Chapter 6 discusses the use of *I* at some length. Use *I* (and other personal pronouns) in your writing whenever it will promote rapid understanding of what you have to say.

i.e. This abbreviation for the Latin *id est* means "that is." When you use it, either set it off as a parenthetical phrase, or place it after a semicolon. And never use it just to show off. That simply wastes words. Compare:

Right.   The man (*i.e.,* Sergeant Boyd) entered the tent.

Better.   Sergeant Boyd entered the tent.

Right.   The second order, *i.e.,* OPORD 8-94, was released to the squad.

Better.   OPORD 8-94 was released to the squad.

Wrong.   A lot of people in this group have left the country, *i.e.,* they have returned to CONUS.

Right.   A lot of people in this group have left the country; *i.e.,* they have returned to CONUS.

Better.   A lot of people in this group have returned to CONUS.

if, whether. Use *if* as a subordinating conjunction to introduce a condition. For example:

If the new survey officer continues to get position data that quickly, he'll even have time to survey the alternate site.

Soldiers will endure a lot of hardship, *if* you lead them well.

When you want to ask an indirect question or show doubt, you should use *whether.* Examples:

> Captain Ptolemy does not know *whether* his orders have been cut.

> The Captain has a plan, but he doesn't know *whether* it will work.

Note: In that last example, the words *or not* might well have been added. But why? They add nothing to the meaning, but they do add length to the text. Get out of the habit of writing *whether or not. Whether* by itself means the same thing.

imminent, eminent. *Imminent* means about to happen; *eminent* means above others, distinguished. To illustrate the difference:

> Admiral Bickerstaff is an *eminent* commander, whose *imminent* return to sea duty is eagerly anticipated at all levels.

imperative mood. This form of the verb is used to direct, command, and request. In most cases its subject will be implied rather than expressed. Here are some examples:

> Attention!

> Fire!

> Straighten your ties.

> Be ready to move out at dawn.

imply, infer. Frequently confused, these words mean two different things. To *imply* is to suggest or hint at; to *infer* is to conclude. Readers draw *inferences* from your *implications.* Examples:

> This report *implies* nothing about the two units that made up the reserve force for the operation. In that case, we can *infer* nothing about either unit.

in, into, in to. You won't confuse *in* and *into* if you'll remember that *in,* literally or figuratively, tells location; *into* tells direction. Examples:

Since getting his orders home, Lieutenant Jacques has had his head *in* the clouds.

Every day we can expect to meet *in* the captain's mess for lunch.

Not until the last trooper got *into* his truck did Captain Sidney get *into* his own jeep.

Sergeant Smith headed *into* town five minutes behind the advance party.

Whenever you use the adverb *in* with the preposition *to* (when that *to* is part of an infinitive), the proper spelling is *in to*. *In to* does not mean the same thing as *into*. Compare these examples:

The two exhausted sailors came *in to* sit by the heater.

Since the gym is nearby, many of troops stop *in to* exercise during the early afternoon.

Failing to make guard mount is a great way to get *into* trouble.

indicative mood. This form of the verb is used to make statements and ask questions. Most of what you write is in the indicative mood. Generally, both subject and verb are present in this form.

indirect discourse. As an alternative to quotation, indirect discourse allows you to paraphrase. That, in turn, can save you words, time, and space. Unless quoting is essential to what you're writing, opt for indirect discourse. For example:

Direct.	Captain Simmel said, "I should be back by 2000 hours. If for some reason I am delayed, stay at your post. I'll get here eventually. And when I do, I'll relieve you." [32 words]
Indirect.	Even if unable to return by 2000 hours, Captain Simmel still promised to relieve the guard when he did get back. [21 words]

indirect objects. Distinguish indirect objects from direct objects by remembering that indirect objects are the thing or person something is said, shown, or given to. Examples:

> The colonel gave *Specialist Cortez* the Army Achievement Medal.

> The operations officer showed *them* his plan.

infinitives. In modern English, infinitives consist of the root form of the verb preceded by the preposition *to*. Infinitives can exist in both the active voice (e.g., *to fight, to have fought*) and passive voice (e.g., *to be fought, to have been fought*); they also exist in the present tense (e.g., *to support*) and the perfect tense (e.g., *to have supported*).

Though they are verb forms, infinitives can also function as subjects, objects, and modifiers. Their greatest use to the military writer is in absolute constructions (i.e., words or phrases that modify an entire sentence). Here are a few examples:

> To win the air-land battle, the fighting forces must take occasional risks.

> To return the enemy's fire effectively, two platoons of howitzers occupied a new position four miles to the northwest.

> To deal fairly with indebtedness, commanders need to have great patience and a sense of fair play.

Note: You might be tempted to prefix any of those sentences with the phrase *in order.* Don't yield to it.

Split infinitives—infinitives with a modifier between the *to* and the root of the verb—will get you into trouble with some readers. Although the revulsion to split infinitives that once existed seems to have diminished somewhat over the last twenty years or so, there are still many people who see them as gross errors. Play it safe: Don't use split infinitives. Examples:

> **Wrong.** The battery clerk makes it his business *to eagerly come* to the orderly room.

> **Right.** The battery clerk makes it his business *to come eagerly* to the orderly room.

Right.   The battery clerk makes it his business *to come* to the
                    orderly room *eagerly.*

interrogative pronouns. Use these pronouns when asking questions.
They are *who, whom, whose, which,* and *what.*

intransitive verbs. These verbs (e.g., *come, happen, vanish,* etc.) do not
take a direct object.

irregardless. Frequently and wrongly used to mean *regardless,* "irregardless" is not a word. Never use it. Never.

its, it's. There is no reason to confuse these words. *Its* is the genitive case—
that is, the possessive case—of the pronoun *it.* Do not use an apostrophe
with *its.* You don't use one with *his;* don't use one with *its* either.

  It's is a contraction, simply another way of writing *it is.* The apostrophe
does not show possession; rather, it shows that the letter *i* has been omitted.

  Mixing up these two words is a howling error. Compare these for correct usage:

> *It's* about time the ammo truck had *its* radiator bled.

> If the spare radio blows *its* fuses, then *it's* back to the supply room
> before we can continue.

-ize endings. New verbs formed by adding *-ize* to nonverbs generally
duplicate old verbs that don't require duplication. It makes no sense to make
a bastard verb out of *utility* (i.e., *utilize*) when the shorter and plainer verb *use*
already exists in the language. It may take real discipline to do it, but fight the
impulse to create or use verbs that end in *-ize.*

latter, former. These terms can sometimes be confusing. It's usually better
to avoid them altogether. If you're dealing with two things, people, ideas,
places, etc., replace *former* with *first* and *latter* with *last.* If you have more
than two, *last* can still replace *latter;* you may identify the other elements as
first, second, etc.

lay, lie. *Lay* is a transitive verb meaning to place or set: You lay something
down. *Lie* is intransitive and means to stretch out as in bed. The confusion in

the two words derives from the spelling of their principal parts. Here's the difference:

Present	Past	Present Participle	Past Participle
lie	lay	lying	lain
lay	laid	laying	laid

Note: Though spelled the same way, the present tense of *lay* and the past tense of *lie* do not mean the same thing.

Lie, when used in the sense of not telling the truth, has different principal parts. They are:

> lie   lied   lying   lied

lead, led. As a noun, *lead* means a soft, heavy metal. The verb *lead* means to direct or guide. *Lead,* the noun, and *lead,* the verb, are not pronounced the same way; the noun and the past tense of the verb, which is *led,* are pronounced the same way. They are not spelled the same way, however. Learn those distinctions if you don't already know them.

lighted, lit. These two words mean the same thing. Both are past-tense forms of the verb *light.* Use *lighted* when it doesn't sound stilted; otherwise, use *lit.* Example:

> **Stilted.**   Have the gas lanterns in the command post been *lighted* yet?

> **Better.**   Have the gas lanterns in the command post been *lit* yet?

like, as. If you have a choice, use *like* rather than *as.* Both words are used in making comparisons. *Like* is most often used as a preposition to introduce a comparison. For example:

> Private Weissmuller swims *like* a fish.

It is less formal than *as.* In making comparisons, *as* is most often used as a conjunction to introduce comparative clauses. To illustrate:

> The new canvas on all the trucks makes them look *as* if they have never spent a day out of garrison.

If you cheat a little and use the informal *like* as a conjunction instead of *as,* you will save a word or two. Consider this:

> The new canvas on all the trucks makes them look *like* they have never spent a day out of garrison.

linking verbs. Verbs that connect a subject and another noun or modifier are linking (or copulative) verbs. More than fifty in number, these words, as their name suggests, express a relationship between the subject and the noun or adjective coming after the verb.

Be is the most common; some of the others are *act, seem, grow, feel, taste, look, sound, prove, smell,* and *appear.*

may, can. *May* asks permission:

> *May* we drop these losses without a report of survey?

or implies a probability, as it does here:

> The unit *may* get orders to move as early as tomorrow.

Can, on the other hand, has to do with ability:

> This airplane *can* carry six passengers back to base camp.

media. *Medium* is the singular form of *media.* Don't make stupid agreement errors by using either word improperly. Examples:

> **Wrong.**   The *media* is not treating the command fairly.
>
> **Right.**   The *media are* not treating the command fairly.

might, could. *Might* is the past tense of *may; could* is the past tense of *can. Might* has to do with permission or probability. *Could* focuses on ability. We frequently use these words in certain constructions in the subjunctive mood. Examples:

> The commander wonders whether we *might* get six more soldiers to augment the battalion for this exercise.

> We asked Captain Standish whether he *could* be in port by sunset, and
> he said yes.

modal auxiliaries. The function of modal auxiliaries is to help other verbs.
They are always used with other verbs, sometimes elliptically. That is, the
verb being helped by the auxiliary may be implied rather than directly
expressed. For instance:

> May we break contact with the enemy? You may not [break contact].

The most common modal auxiliaries are *can, could; may, might; must;
ought; shall, should; will, would.*

modifiers. Words that give more information about other words are called
modifiers. In using them, remember two things. First, see if you can eliminate the need for modifiers by picking more precise nouns and verbs. Then
put modifiers as close as you can to the words and phrases they are supposed
to modify.

money. Two general rules apply when it comes to expressing money. First,
be consistent in your format; second, use common sense. Specifically:

1. Write exact amounts in figures (e.g., $117, $63), round amounts in
words (e.g., three dollars), and a combination of amounts in figures (e.g.,
$117.62, $3.00).
2. Write out amounts when you use them as modifiers (e.g., a six-dollar
manual, a two-hundred-dollar mistake).
3. Write amounts of a million or more as a combination of figures and
words (e.g., $30 million).
4. Though $1.7 million may be many dollars, the amount still takes a
singular verb. Examples:

> **Wrong.**   Two thousand dollars *are* a lot of money for one cam-
> ouflage net.

> **Right.**   Two thousand dollars *is* a lot of money for one camou-
> flage net.

mood. Depending on what you want to do, you may use verbs in three
moods. The indicative mood is the most common. Use it to make statements

and ask questions. Use the subjunctive mood to treat hypothetical situations. To order or direct, use the imperative mood.

Ms. This abbreviation can be used instead of Miss or Mrs. When you don't know which of the three titles is appropriate, you will be correct if you use Ms. Many women, married or not, prefer Ms., and you should be sensitive to that preference.

neither/nor, either/or. Keep two things in mind when using either of these correlative conjunctions. First, *either* and *neither* both take a singular verb. Second, if half the compound subject you use is plural and the other half is singular, your verb must agree with the nearer subject. To illustrate:

> **Wrong.** Neither sick troops nor bad *weather are* enough to justify moving this base.

> **Right.** Neither bad weather nor sick *troops are* enough to justify moving this base.

> **Right.** Neither sick troops nor bad *weather is* enough to justify moving this base.

nominative case. When you look up a noun in the dictionary, you will find it in the singular nominative case. The relative pronoun *who;* the singular personal pronouns *I, you, he, she,* and *it;* and the plural personal pronouns *we, you,* and *they* have distinctive nominative forms.

none. As a pronoun, *none* takes a singular verb when you want to use it in the sense of *not one, no one,* or *no measurable amount.* Examples:

> Of all the Ben Het combat veterans, *none has come* to this reunion.

> When Sergeant Minnes looked on the shelf for cleaning solvent, *none was* there.

But when *none* stands in for two or more things that can be counted, you are on solid ground to use a plural verb. For instance:

> Commander Norbert knew that *none* of his men *were* eager to make a third dive.

When Sergeant Minnes reached for the six ammunition clips, *none were* at hand.

So much for hairsplitting. You may use *none* (like *all, any,* and *some*) to express either an individual or collective sense of the pronoun. Whether you use a singular or plural verb with it will tell your readers the sense you want them to take it in. For example:

None of Sergeant Hollander's instructions *helps* in this situation.

None of Sergeant Hollander's instructions *help* in this situation.

nonsexist language. In trying to avoid sexual stereotyping in language, we often solve one problem by creating another. That is particularly the case in the matter of pronoun-antecedent agreement. People who are sensitive to sexist language but insensitive to good usage write stuff like this:

Wrong.   Everyone should have their tent up by late afternoon.

People sensitive to both sexist language and good usage might instead write:

Right.   Everyone should have *his* or *her* tent up by late afternoon.

Constructions of that sort, though, do little to promote a fast reading. Here are a couple of alternatives:

Better.   *People* should have *their* tents up by late afternoon.

Better.   All tents should be up by late afternoon.

As a general practice, try to use the plural pronouns *their, them,* and *they* (with plural verbs, of course) instead of *he* or *she, he/she, s/he, his/her,* and similarly awkward constructions. That way you reduce the possibility of offending your reader with sexist language, the likelihood of making an agreement error, and the number of words you use.

nor. *Nor* is paired with *neither* when used as a correlative conjunction. Without *neither, nor* is a negative conjunction. Use it when you want to emphasize the negative. Like other conjunctions, *nor* may begin a sentence. Some examples:

> A lot of paperwork doesn't do much for this unit's efficiency, *nor* does it do a whole lot for anyone's morale.

> The captain has withdrawn all shore leaves for this weekend. *Nor* will he approve any for next weekend.

It may also be used to connect the last two elements of a negative series, but that's getting pretty stilted.

not hardly. *Hardly* means "almost surely not." To say *not hardly* is to say "not almost surely not," which is the same thing as saying "almost surely." Don't use *not hardly*.

noun clauses. A dependent clause that performs as a noun is a noun clause. When using noun clauses, pay special attention to agreement. You can use *whether, what, that, which, whatever, why, how,* and other similar words to introduce noun clauses. Some typical examples:

> *How the log book got lost* remains a mystery to Private Snellings.

> Realizing *that his force had regained its momentum,* Captain Smollet renewed the attack.

> *Why marines should engage in regular physical training* is obvious to anyone familiar with their mission.

nouns. Nouns are words that name people, places, and things. They exist in proper and common forms. Proper nouns are the names of particular people, places, and things (e.g., George Armstrong Custer, Fort Bliss, *Old Ironsides*) and require capitalization. All other nouns are common. Nouns may also be concrete (e.g., rifle, tent) or abstract (e.g., fidelity, valor).

In sentences, use nouns as subjects, direct objects, indirect objects, appositives, and complements (see separate entries for each).

number. Like *all, any, none,* and *some, number* takes either a singular or plural verb, depending on what you want it to mean. If you want it to mean *a few, some,* or *many,* use a plural verb. For example:

A *number* of the cooks *were* absent from the noon formation.

If you want *number* read to mean one unit, use a singular verb. For example:

The *number* of Colonel Perkins's ribbons *is* worth noting the next time you see him.

numbers. Common sense and consistency are your anchors when using figures. Here are a few specific guidelines:

1. Don't begin a sentence with a figure; rather, write out the number. Example:

Eight new men reported for duty this afternoon.

2. Always write out the numbers one through ten. In formal writing, write out the numbers one through a hundred.

3. Do not engage in the pointless practice of writing out numbers and following them with figures in parentheses. In other words, don't do this:

Six (6) men received *six* (6) awards for *six* (6) acts of heroism.

4. Write out even numbers (e.g., two hundred, six thousand).

5. Do not mix words and figures in the same series. Examples:

Wrong.   We need *six* cases of grenades, *12* new spools of telephone wire, *four* pounds of lime, and *229* mess trays.

Right.   We need *6* cases of grenades, *12* new spools of telephone wire, *4* pounds of lime, and 229 mess trays.

6. Hyphenate two-word numbers from twenty-one through ninety-nine.

objects. Three kinds of objects need your attention. The simplest to recognize is the direct object of a transitive verb. Most times, the direct object receives the action of the verb. Many times the direct object will be a noun or a pronoun; it can also be a noun phrase. A few examples:

The new chief greeted *his section.*

Our troops despise *moving in the rain.*

Indirect objects are a little more complicated but still easy enough to deal with. They are the person, place, or thing indirectly affected by the verbal action. Some examples:

Captain Shears wrote *Captain Blades* a long letter.

Running for more than ten miles each day gave *the troops* time for little else.

The noun or noun phrase that follows a preposition is the object of the preposition. The object, along with the preposition, must modify another element in the sentence. For example:

Before they surrendered, the three soldiers hid *for two days.*

In this case, *two days* is the object of the preposition *for.* Together those two elements make up a prepositional phrase whose function is to modify the verb *hid.*

on, onto, on to. Depending on style and tone, *on* and *onto* are sometimes used interchangeably in the sense of "to a place on." Examples:

The door gunner climbed *on* the skid.

The door gunner climbed *onto* the skid.

In both examples, *on* and *onto* are prepositions. When *onto* is a preposition, write it as one word; when *on* is an adverb working with the preposition *to,* write them as two words. Example:

The tank pulled *on to* the hardstand.

So how can you tell the difference? Easy. The sense here is actually "The tank pulled on [a little farther] to the hardstand." If *hardstand* were the object of *on,* then *on* would have to be a preposition. But *hardstand* is the object of the preposition *to.* In this example, *to* is a preposition and *on* an adverb. *On* and *to,* then, must be written as two words.

one of those who. This construction will trip you up, so be alert when using it. The antecedent of the relative pronoun *who* (or *that* when you write *one of those that*) is *those*. *Those* is plural and, therefore, takes a plural verb. Some examples:

Wrong.	Bravo thirteen is one of *those* trucks that *runs* poorly in cold weather.
Right.	Bravo thirteen is one of *those* trucks that *run* poorly in cold weather.
Right.	Bravo thirteen is one *truck* that *runs* poorly in cold weather.
Wrong.	Lieutenant Mutto is one of *those* who *needs* more practice with the new fire direction system.
Right.	Lieutenant Mutto is one of *those* who *need* more practice with the new fire direction system.

only. Where you place the word *only* in a sentence is a matter of some importance. Look at these six examples:

Sergeant Bradley cares *only* about running a good aid station.

Only Sergeant Bradley cares about running a good aid station.

Sergeant Bradley *only* cares about running a good aid station.

Sergeant Bradley cares about running a good aid station *only.*

Sergeant Bradley cares about running *only* a good aid station.

Sergeant Bradley cares about *only* running a good aid station.

As you can see, the placement of *only* affects how you read each of these sentences. Be sure you know what you want to modify with *only* before you use it. The surest way to have it understood as you want it to be is to put *only* in front of the word or phrase you intend to modify.

or. Like other coordinating conjunctions, *or* (preceded by a comma) joins independent clauses together. You may begin sentences with *or,* but that often makes readers uneasy. And you may use it to connect shorter grammatical units of equal weight. When you use *or* that way, pay particular attention to agreement. In mixed constructions, the verb must agree with the subject element closest to it. Examples:

> A new grenade launcher *or* a new *rifle is* provided to each squad.

> Two new grenade launchers *or* a new *rifle is* provided to each squad.

> Two new grenade launchers *or* two new *rifles are* provided to each squad.

> A new grenade launcher *or* two new *rifles are* provided to each squad.

paragraphs. In military writing, paragraphs shouldn't be more than three to six sentences long. Those sentences must relate to each other and contribute to the overall flow of the document they're a part of. Your reader needs to know what your paragraphs are about. To that end, you must either write good topic sentences or use effective headings (see chapter 5).

Paragraphs must be identified as paragraphs. The usual way is to indent the first line. If you aren't working within a prescribed format, double-space between paragraphs.

Sometimes a one-sentence paragraph can be quite effective.

Other times, as you see here, one-sentence paragraphs can be quite annoying.

parallelism. Elements whose grammatical functions are similar must have parallel constructions. Compare these examples.

Wrong.	Our maintenance programs have the advantage of saving soldiers time, their energy, and keeping them from repeating the same tasks.
Right.	Our maintenance programs have the advantage of saving soldiers time, energy, and effort.
Wrong.	The operations order calls for camping early and also to eat early.

Right.	The operations order calls for early camping and eating.

paraphrase. As an alternative to direct quotation, you may restate someone else's words in your own. Your paraphrase must contain all of the information in the original version. It should also be considerably shorter.

parentheses. Like commas and dashes, parentheses are used to separate certain material from the rest of a sentence. Usually the things you put in parentheses will be almost an aside to the rest of the sentence. Most of the time you won't use parentheses in military writing; when you do use them, the material they enclose is likely to be explanatory. Some examples:

For purposes of this exercise, the direction of fire *(600 mils for Battery A; 800 mils for Battery B; 1100 mils for Battery C)* is not a matter of choice.

Our casualties for this operation *(six wounded),* though light, remain a source of continued concern.

Two awards, an Air Force Commendation Medal to Airman Joseph J. Paul *(valor)* and the Joint Service Medal to Captain Wellington M. Pizarro *(meritorious achievement),* need your approval.

Instructions in the duty officer's SOP *(ch. 6, para. 4-1 and para. 8; ch. 9, para. 11-2)* are emphatic on the procedures for calling an alert.

As several of these examples show, judicious use of parentheses can save you a fair number of words. By the same token, you can use them to add a lot of unnecessary material as well. When you use them, keep that difference in mind.

participles. Though derived from verbs, participles cannot stand alone as predicates. Examples:

Wrong.	The battle plan *being* set.
Right.	The battle plan *is* set.
Wrong.	The troops *eating* their dinner in the mess hall.
Right.	The troops *are eating* their dinner in the mess hall.

Right. The troops *eat* their dinner in the mess hall.

Participles exist in these four forms:

	Present Participle	**Past Participle**
Active Voice	starting	started
Passive Voice	being started	having been started

They function as verbal modifiers and, as such, may be used in a variety of ways. One of the most common is as an introduction to the rest of a sentence. In using introductory participles, be careful not to leave them dangling. Compare these examples:

Wrong.   *Firing the rifle on automatic,* the weapon's recoil was painful to Private Kelley.

Right.   *Firing his rifle on automatic,* Private Kelley was painfully aware of the weapon's recoil.

Wrong.   *Having understood the requirement,* there was no reason for Commander Tracey to remain at the meeting any longer.

Right.   *Having understood the requirement,* Commander Tracey saw no reason to stay at the meeting any longer.

Participles may also be used as simple modifiers. Some illustrations:

the *sleeping* sailors

a *borrowed* uniform

the *jamming* rifle

his *broken* transmission

their *burning* powder

Introductory participial phrases are absolute constructions that seem to have only general relationship to the rest of a sentence. If not worked to death, they can be quite useful, particularly in making a transition from one thought to another or in summing up. Some examples:

Depending on the situation, we may be directed to attack as early as noon tomorrow.

All things considered, this operation has been pretty successful.

Use the present participle and a form of the verb *to be* to form progressive tenses. Examples:

The woodline *is* still *smoking* from yesterday's air strike.

People *were running* toward the waterpoint at breakneck speed.

The past participle with a form of the verb *to be* forms the passive voice. Sometimes the passive is appropriate, but most of the time you should make a conscious effort to avoid constructions like these:

The order *has been received.*

Our position *has been occupied.*

parts of speech. Parts of speech are categories grammarians use to classify the different words we use. These classifications do not last for all time, nor are they necessarily the same, in all cases, for all grammarians. There is far more to say on this subject than you will probably ever want or need to know.

Basically, there are seven parts of speech a military writer needs to know about and be able to use effectively. Each is dealt with in more detail elsewhere in this section. Here, suffice it to name these parts of speech and define them briefly.

1. Nouns: words that name people, places, and things
2. Pronouns: words that stand in for nouns
3. Verbs: words that show action
4. Adjectives: words that modify nouns
5. Adverbs: words that modify verbs, adjectives, and other adverbs
6. Prepositions: words that relate a noun or pronoun to another element of a sentence

7. Conjunctions: words that connect different elements of a sentence

passive voice. Military writers need to make a special effort to avoid writing in the passive voice. Getting out of the passive voice isn't easy, because it is so common in military prose. A form of the verb *to be* and the past participle of the main verb combine to create the passive voice.

The main weakness of the passive voice is that it hides the actor and focuses on the action instead. Usually that's a poor way to communicate, because much important information is not obvious to the reader. Of course, when the actor really isn't important, you wouldn't be incorrect to use the passive voice. Keep in mind, though, that the passive voice tends to be wordier than the active voice. These examples illustrate that point:

Passive.	The study that *was conducted* by the operations officer has been received by the commander.
Active.	The commander *has received* the operations officer's study.
Passive.	Most of the firing *had been done* by myself.
Active.	I *did* most of the firing.
Passive.	The rifle *was lost* by Private Lucretius.
Active.	Private Lucretius *lost* the rifle.

past tense. *Passive voice* and *past tense* are not the same thing. The passive voice cannot exist without some form of the verb *to be* in combination with the past participle. The past tense simply adds *ed* to all regular verbs. Don't confuse those two forms. Examples:

Past tense.	The mess sergeant *baked* the bread.
Passive voice.	The bread *has been baked* by the mess sergeant.

per. This Latin word means through, among, etc. Some military writers use it to mean according to or in accordance with. That's bad usage. Even so, if you must use either *in accordance with* or *per,* by all means go with *per.* Your best choice, though, is to use neither and simply get on with saying whatever it is you need to say.

percent. In all but the most formal writing, you may use *percent* rather than proportion or percentage. *Percent,* when functioning as a collective noun, will, like *number,* take either a singular or plural verb, depending on the sense you want to convey. Examples:

> A large *percent* of the battalion *has* had flu shots.

> A large *percent* of the battalion *have* had flu shots.

perfect tense. The three perfect tenses—present perfect, past perfect, and future perfect—are all formed with the past participle and some form of the verb *to have.* Examples:

> **Present perfect.** Our destroyer *has left* port.

> **Past perfect.** Our destroyer *had left* port.

> **Future perfect.** Our destroyer *will have left* port.

period. The most common terminal punctuation mark is the period. Because it is so common, military writers sometimes forget to use question marks when they should, in fact, be used. Don't make that mistake.

When using standard abbreviations such as *Dr.* and *etc.,* follow them with a period. Military abbreviations such as NATO and MAJ do not take a period.

If the last word of a sentence is inside quotation marks, put the period inside the quotation marks as well—even though the period is not part of the quotation.

periodic sentences. Periodic sentences are great in speeches and essays but are generally to be avoided in military writing. Why? Because they withhold their meaning until the last word or clause. That sort of suspense can be extremely effective; it can also be extremely vexing for someone who is trying to read and understand quickly.

If you feel compelled to write periodic sentences from time to time, you might write them along the lines suggested by these examples:

> After many weeks of intensive physical activity, emotional strain, mental exhaustion, and deprivation of all but the most elemental creature comforts, these young men, some of whom had never traveled more

than a hundred miles from home, could say one thing, and say it proudly: They were Marines.

Moved as I am by your many arguments, my sense of things, particularly in view of our present situation, forces me to say no to your request for leave.

But if you write such sentences, recognize that you are trading economy and efficiency for rhetorical effect. Be sure the little bit of drama a periodic sentence adds is worth the high price of using it.

person. This grammatical term refers to verb inflection and pronoun classification. For both verbs and pronouns, person takes six different forms: first-, second-, and third-person singular; first-, second-, and third-person plural. The first person is the one speaking (I, me, my, we, us, our). The second person is the one spoken to (you, your, yours). The third person is anyone else (he, him, his, she, her, hers, it, its, they, them, their).

personal pronouns. Personal pronouns exist in singular and plural forms. They also have forms in three persons (first, second, and third) and in three cases (nominative, genitive, and accusative). Here's the breakdown:

	First Person	
Case	**Singular**	**Plural**
nominative	I	we
genitive	my, mine	our, ours
accusative	me	us

	Second Person	
Case	**Singular**	**Plural**
nominative	you	you
genitive	your, yours	your, yours
accusative	you	you

	Third Person	
Case	**Singular**	**Plural**
nominative	he, she, it	they
genitive	his; her, hers; its	their, theirs
accusative	him, her, it	them

Note: None of these pronouns, even the ones that end with *s,* takes an apostrophe. If you have questions, see the entry for *its, it's.*

phenomena. The plural of *phenomenon* is *phenomena.* As a plural noun it takes a plural verb. For example:

> Two *phenomena* associated with a well-trained army *are* the soldiers' ability to endure deprivation and their resolve in the face of even the most powerful enemies.

phrasal verbs. Any verb combining a main verb with an auxiliary verb is a phrasal verb (e.g., *was searching, will retreat, has been promoted*).

phrase. A phrase can be a group of words that functions as the subject or object of a sentence. Or it may be a group of words (without a subject or predicate) that modifies some other element of a sentence. Broadly, there are four kinds of phrases: gerund, infinitive, prepositional, and participial.

Gerund phrases function only as subjects or objects. These phrases consist of a gerund, its object, and any modifiers. The phrase "Sergeant Thompson's firing" has no object. "Sergeant Thompson's firing the rifle" does. Here's an illustration of how a gerund phrase works in a sentence:

> *Sergeant Thompson's firing the rifle* was the thing that turned the attack around.

In that example the gerund phrase is the subject of the sentence; in this one, it's the object:

> The thing that turned the attack around was *Sergeant Thompson's firing the rifle.*

Infinitive phrases function as subjects and objects but also as modifiers. These phrases consist of an infinitive, its object, and any modifiers. "To fire quickly" is an infinitive phrase without an object; "to fire the rifle quickly" has an object. These examples show how infinitives work in sentences:

> **As modifier.** *To fire the rifle quickly,* Sergeant Thompson practiced every day.

As subject.   *To fire the rifle quickly* was Sergeant Thompson's specialty.

As object.   Sergeant Thompson chose *to fire the rifle quickly.*

Prepositional phrases function only as modifiers. They consist of a
preposition and its object. As modifiers, prepositional phrases can be both
adverbs and adjectives. For example:

As adverb.   When the mortars started to impact *on the perimeter,* the
marines ran *into their bunkers.*

As adjective.   After the shelling, they replaced two strands *of wire* and
put out another case *of claymores.*

Participial phrases function only as modifiers. Frequently used to
introduce sentences, these phrases consist of either the present or past participle, its object, and any modifiers. "Training the troops vigorously" has an
object; "training vigorously" does not. Compare:

Training the troops vigorously, Sergeant Thompson is becoming
increasingly proficient himself.

Sergeant Thompson, *training vigorously,* sets a superb example for the
other NCOs.

plurals. Plurals of most English nouns are formed by adding *s.* Enough are
not, though, to cause problems for some writers. You can solve the majority
of those problems by following these rules:

1. Form plurals of nouns ending in *-ch, -sh, -s,* and *-z* by adding *-es.*
2. Form plurals of nouns ending in *-y* preceded by a consonant (e.g.,
lady, body, etc.) by dropping the *-y* and adding *-ies.*
3. Form plurals of nouns ending in *-o* preceded by a vowel by adding *-s.*
4. Form plurals of most nouns ending in *-o* preceded by a consonant by
adding *-s.*
5. Form plurals of some nouns ending in *-o* preceded by a consonant
(e.g., *hero, mosquito,* etc.) by adding *-es.*
6. Form plurals of some nouns ending in *-f* or *-fe* (e.g., *half, knife,* etc.)
by dropping the ending and adding *-ves.*

7. Form plurals of some nouns ending in *-f* simply by adding *-s*.

8. Form plurals of certain Anglo-Saxon words by changing a vowel (e.g., *woman, women*) or the ending (e.g., *child, children*).

9. Form plurals of certain Latinate words by changing *-um* endings to *-a* (e.g., *medium, media*), *-on* endings to *-a* (e.g., *phenomenon, phenomena*), and *-us* endings to *-i* (e.g., *alumnus, alumni*).

Most of the time, forming plurals is a pretty straightforward process. You can take advantage of that by learning these nine rules and by looking up any words you aren't sure about. If the plural form you seek is nonstandard, the dictionary will provide it. Otherwise, follow the rule that applies to the word at issue.

possessive adjectives. The personal pronouns *my, your, his, her, its,* and *our* are sometimes called possessive adjectives when they function as modifiers (e.g., *my* track, *our* ship, *his* map, etc.).

possessive case. The possessive or genitive case is used to show possession. "The boots of the marine" shows possession; so does, "the marine's boots." When you have a choice, use *'s* to show possession.

Show singular possession by using an *'s;* show plural possession by using *s'*. Examples:

> officer's hat
> hat of the officer
> officers' hats
> hats of the officers

possessive pronouns. *Whose* is the possessive form of the relative pronoun *who*. The possessive forms of the personal pronouns are *my, mine; your, yours; his, her, hers, its; our, ours;* and *their, theirs*.

predicate. The verb with all its modifiers, objects, or complements is the predicate of a sentence. Its function is to comment in some way on the subject.

predominant, predominate. Military writers frequently confuse these words. The adjective *predominant* means having the most authority or prevalent. *Predominate* is a verb meaning to be most outstanding or to prevail. Compare:

In the early phases of the operation the marines were the *predominant* force; by day's end, however, the Air Force *predominated* the battlefield.

prepositional phrase. Functioning either as an adjective or adverb, a prepositional phrase consists of a preposition and its object. Examples:

> **Adjectival.**   The aircraft *with its eager crew* took off at dawn.

> **Adverbial.**   The position was secured *by two mechanized infantry companies.*

prepositions. A preposition relates a noun or a pronoun to some other part of a sentence. Writers seldom have trouble using prepositions effectively unless they try to use too many in the same sentence. You can avoid that problem by keeping your sentences about fifteen words long.

Some writers agonize over trying not to end a sentence with a preposition. Unless you are writing the most formal kind of document, don't worry about it. You needn't go out of your way to end sentences with prepositions either. Given a choice, though, go for fewer words. Compare:

> Captain Adams is the officer *with* whom I spoke. [9 words]

> Captain Adams is the officer I spoke *with*. [8 words]

principal, principle. As an adjective, *principal* means first or foremost. *Principal,* the noun, means the main person or thing. *Principle* is also a noun meaning precept or idea. Don't confuse these words by misspelling them. Compare:

> General Wiggens, at one time a school *principal* and now the *principal* speaker of the conference, spoke on the *principles* of military discipline.

principal parts of verbs. The infinitive, past tense, and past participle are the principal parts of a verb. Regular (or weak) verbs are easy to deal with: To get the past tense and past participle, simply add *ed* to the infinitive (e.g., *polish, polished, polished; talk, talked, talked;* etc.).

The irregular (or strong) verbs, depending on how they happened to come into the language, form their principal parts in a variety of ways. Some change a vowel; some change the final consonant; some don't change at all. The best way to manage the principal parts of irregular verbs is to memorize them. Some of the more common ones are printed below. For the principal parts of others, consult a decent dictionary.

Infinitive	Past Tense	Past Participle
be	was	been
begin	began	begun
bite	bit	bitten
blow	blew	blown
break	broke	broken
bring	brought	brought
choose	chose	chosen
come	came	come
cost	cost	cost
dig	dug	dug
dive	dived *or* dove	dived
do	did	done
drink	drank	drunk
drive	drove	driven
eat	ate	eaten
fall	fell	fallen
fly	flew	flown
forget	forgot	forgot *or* forgotten
freeze	froze	frozen
get	got	got *or* gotten
give	gave	given
go	went	gone
hear	heard	heard
know	knew	known
lay	laid	laid
lead	led	led
lie	lay	lain
lose	lost	lost
ride	rode	ridden
ring	rang	rung
rise	rose	risen

Infinitive	Past Tense	Past Participle
run	ran	run
see	saw	seen
shine	shined *or* shone	shined *or* shone
slide	slid	slid
speak	spoke	spoken
steal	stole	stolen
swim	swam	swum
swing	swung	swung
take	took	taken
throw	threw	thrown
wake	woke	waked *or* woken
wear	wore	worn
write	wrote	written

prior to. A long-time favorite with military writers, this annoying phrase means before. When tempted to write *prior to,* be strong and write *before* instead.

progressive verb forms. Verb phrases made with the present participle and some form of the verb *to be* are known as progressive verb forms. Sometimes the sense of what you need to communicate requires you to use them; other times it doesn't. Progressive forms, like the passive voice, use more words. For example, "they are eating" uses one more word than "they eat." When you don't need the sense of meaning conveyed by the progressive form, don't use it.

pronouns. Words that can replace nouns and perform the same grammatical functions they perform are called pronouns. Military writers sometimes have trouble with them, because many pronouns have different forms in the nominative, genitive, and accusative cases. The only real solution to that problem is to learn the forms.

There are eight kinds of pronouns. **Personal pronouns,** perhaps the most familiar, show person, number, and gender; in the genitive case, they function as **possessive pronouns.**

Reflexive pronouns are pronouns combined with the ending *-self* to form words (e.g., *myself, themselves,* etc.) that refer to and emphasize the subject. **Relative pronouns**—*that, which,* and *who*—introduce dependent clauses that modify another element of a sentence.

The four **demonstrative pronouns** (*this, that, these,* and *those*) show or point back to specific material. When using them, make sure that what they refer to is clear to your reader.

Reciprocal pronouns—*each other* and *one another*—take the place of compound or plural subjects in the objective position.

There are five **interrogative pronouns:** *what, which, who, whom,* and *whose.* Use them the same way you use other interrogatives (e.g., *how, when, where, why,* etc.): to ask direct and indirect questions.

Indefinite pronouns will cause you little trouble except in the area of subject-verb agreement. When you use one of these pronouns—e.g., *somebody, anyone, nothing, either, each,* etc.—as a subject, you must use a singular verb. Depending on the sense you want to convey, other indefinite pronouns—e.g., *all, none, some,* etc.—can take either a singular verb (e.g., All is well) or a plural verb (e.g., None have been on this road before).

provided, providing. Both of these words are used as a conditional connective to mean "as long as." For example:

> You may turn in your shelter half *provided* it is clean.

> You may turn in your shelter half *providing* it is clean.

If you have to use either, use *provided.* Better still, write this:

> You may turn in your shelter half *if* it is clean.

punctuation. Make no mistake about it: There are some fairly rigid rules governing punctuation. In the main, you should abide by them in the interest of producing writing that can be understood in a single rapid reading. If you keep your constructions short, simple, and to the point, you won't have many punctuation problems—almost by definition. Here's a quick review:

1. Sentences must end with a terminal punctuation mark, i.e., a period, question mark, or exclamation point.

2. Independent clauses must be separated by a coordinating conjunction preceded by a comma, a semicolon, a colon, or a conjunctive adverb preceded by a semicolon and followed by a comma.

3. Dependent clauses, introductory phrases over five words long, and the different elements (except the last) of a series must be followed by a comma.

4. A nonrestrictive dependent clause following a main clause must be preceded by a comma.

5. Nonrestrictive modifiers (that is, modifiers that can fall out of a sentence without killing it) must be set off by commas.

6. Parenthetical elements must be set off by commas, dashes, or parentheses.

punctuation of possessives. Show possession by using the genitive case (e.g., the rifle of the soldier), an 's (e.g., the soldier's rifle), or s' (e.g., the soldiers' rifles). Try to use 's (or s') whenever you can.

quasi-. This Latin word means "to a degree." It is prefixed to a noun, adjective, or adverb to create a new word with the sense of "looks like but not really." If you don't overwork it, it can be useful. Sometimes it's just what you need. For example:

> The colonel strongly disapproves of civilian groups using quasi-military training.

And it is one way to save words. Compare:

> The company looked like it was competent, but it wasn't.

> The company was quasi-competent.

Before you go creating words like that, though, be sure you really need to. They can be pretty awful.

question mark. One of three terminal punctuation marks, the question mark is used at the end of a direct question, but not at the end of indirect questions. Examples:

> **Direct.** The first mate asked, "May I go below, sir?"

> **Indirect.** The first mate asked whether he might go below.

quotation marks. Frequently confused with italics, these punctuation marks are primarily used to report the words of someone other than the writer. On those rare occasions when you may have to record a quotation within a quotation, use single quotation marks within double quotation marks. Here's an example:

> Commodore Bantam said, "My opinion is 'Damn the torpedoes,' but I
> know that sort of abandon has obvious risks."

When using other punctuation marks in conjunction with quotation marks, follow these conventions: periods and commas go inside quotation marks; semicolons and colons go outside; question marks and exclamation marks go either inside or outside, depending on whether the entire sentence or just the part of it that is quoted is a question or an exclamation. Compare these examples:

> Is there time, as our British visitor put it, "to chat them up"?

> The recruit asked, "When is it time to sack out?"

Use quotation marks to enclose titles of essays, articles, songs, marches, etc. Book titles and foreign words must be in italics (underline on a typewriter).

raise, rear. These words usually aren't confused except in the sense of bringing up children. In that context, *rear* is the proper term, though many people use *raise* instead. Parents *rear* children; farmers *raise* cattle. There is a difference.

real, really. Both of these modifiers are amplifiers; both are overworked. *Real* is the adjective, and *really* is the adverb. Though some regional dialects use *real* as an adverb—"come back *real* soon"—don't use it in your writing.

reciprocal pronouns. *Each other* and *one another* are reciprocal pronouns. Use the first pair when you are dealing with two people, places, or things; use the second when talking about three or more. In the objective position these pronouns replace compound or plural subjects. Examples:

> As staff officers, Major Saddler and Colonel Wells complement *each other.*

> The platoon members recognized *one another* immediately.

redundancy. Military writers are particularly susceptible to being redundant—probably because they try so hard to be exact. In writing, keep this in mind: Saying something two or three times does not make it more substantial than it already is. Repetition will not make an absolute more absolute. This example:

> Sergeant Wilbye's one-of-a-kind opportunity was most unique.

overkills this point:

> Sergeant Wilbye's opportunity was unique.

reference of pronouns. Two pronoun-reference problems dog military writers on a pretty regular basis. One occurs when a writer uses a singular antecedent and a plural pronoun or a plural antecedent and a singular pronoun. The second occurs when the antecedent of the pronoun isn't clearly apparent.

You can overcome this first problem by paying attention to what you're talking about. Particularly, you have to be careful that prepositional phrases don't lead you astray. For example:

> **Wrong.**   The *crate* of projectiles lost *their* shipping band.

> **Right.**   The *crate* of projectiles lost *its* shipping band.

Collective nouns will also lead you into making agreement errors if you aren't consistent. For instance:

> **Wrong.**   *Company C* has improved its maintenance record and *their* requisitioning procedures.

> **Right.**   *Company C* has improved *its* maintenance record and *its* requisitioning procedures.

> **Better.**   *Company C* has improved *its* maintenance record and requisitioning procedures.

An obvious solution to the second problem is to put pronouns near their antecedents. One thing that will force you to do that is putting a limit of fifteen words on your sentences. Consider these illustrations:

> **Wrong.**   Until the brigade headquarters approve the battalion's plan and releases *their* funds, *they* have no hope of getting this operation in motion.

Right.   If *they* want to get this operation in motion, the brigade headquarters must release *their* funds and approve the battalion's plan.

In the first example, the reader cannot be sure what *their* and *they* refer to. In the second, it is clear that *their* and *they* refer to the brigade headquarters. The revised sentence still needs editing, though. For instance:

Better.   The brigade headquarters can get this operation moving by releasing their funds and approving the battalion's plan.

reflexive pronouns. Used to clarify or emphasize, the reflexive pronouns are *myself, yourself, himself, herself, itself, ourselves, yourselves,* and *themselves.* Prompted by the fear of misusing personal pronouns in the first-person singular, many writers replace *I* and *me* with *myself.* As a rule, that's a bad idea. Don't do it. It makes no sense to write:

They spoke to no one but Captain Holmes and *myself.*

instead of:

They spoke to Captain Holmes and *me.*

relative clauses. Sometimes called adjectival clauses, relative clauses immediately follow the nouns they modify. They are introduced by relative pronouns or adverbs such as *hence, when, whence, where,* and *why.* In the interest of saving words, you can sometimes omit the introductory relative pronoun. For example:

Private Weelkes worked for two hours on a race ring *that he knew he couldn't fix.*

Private Weelkes worked for two hours on a race ring *he knew he couldn't fix.*

Likewise, you can sometimes drop the relative adverb. For instance:

The two airmen went back to the place *where they came from.*

The two airmen went back to the place *they came from.*

If you start leaving out those introductory elements, be sure you aren't sacrificing clarity and precision for brevity. When in doubt, include the relative pronoun or adverb with the rest of the clause.

relative pronouns. You need not be confused by relative pronouns if you know which ones refer to what. Here's the rule: *who, whom,* and *whose* refer to persons; *that* refers to things. *Whose* may also be used with things. Examples:

> Here's a report *whose* purpose is unclear.

> A gauge *whose* pressure indicators are uncalibrated is unreliable at best.

restrictive modifiers. Restrictive modifiers limit or restrict the nouns they modify; hence, they are not separated by commas from the nouns they modify. Restrictive modifiers are essential to the meaning of the sentences they appear in. Their function is to identify precisely the nouns they modify.

Nonrestrictive modifiers, on the other hand, add nice-to-know information, but it is not essential to the meaning of the sentences they appear in. They are separated from the nouns they modify by commas. Some examples:

Restrictive.	The soldier *who fired the first round* is in my squad.
Nonrestrictive.	Private Bowles, *the soldier who fired the first round,* is in my squad.
Restrictive.	The four marines *who had their liberty revoked* came from Norfolk.
Nonrestrictive.	Privates Adams, Andrews, Smythe, and Worthing, *four marines who had their liberty revoked,* came from Norfolk.

In the first example, the restrictive modifier is the thing that identifies (i.e., restricts, limits) the soldier. In the second example, his name does that job; that he fired the first round is no longer essential information in our identification of the soldier. Likewise, the restrictive modifier *who had their liberty revoked* is the thing that limits the four marines—and makes it clear which four we're talking about. But in the fourth example, that information is no longer needed to restrict the noun.

rhetorical questions. Inexperienced writers sometimes confuse rhetorical questions with substantive evidence. Don't make that mistake. A rhetorical question does not expect an answer; indeed, the reader has no forum for a response even if she has an answer to it. Though rhetorical questions have been around for a very long time, they really have no place in military writing.

run-on sentences. Chapter 7 goes into some detail about the run-on sentence. This error occurs when writers join independent clauses without using the right coordination or punctuation. Some examples:

Wrong.	The retreat ceremony began on time Major Custis was late.
Right.	The retreat ceremony began on time, and Major Custis was late.
Wrong.	The retreat ceremony began on time, however, Major Custis was late.
Right.	The retreat ceremony began on time; however, Major Custis was late.
Wrong.	The retreat ceremony began on time, Major Custis was late.
Right.	The retreat ceremony began on time; Major Custis was late.

semi-. Used as a prefix to form new words, *semi-* means half, less than fully, or twice within a given period. Some examples:

News of his unexpected promotion left Corporal Watson in a *semistupor.*

The platoon's position is only *semiorganized.*

These *semiannual* inspections may become quarterly inspections.

Before you get in the business of creating a lot of new words with this prefix, make sure you really need them. Most of the words you create with it won't be very good, in any case.

semicolon. This strange little punctuation mark rarely turns up in military prose, because most military writers haven't got a clue as to its proper use. These rules may help:

1. You must use a semicolon to precede conjunctive adverbs such as *however* and *moreover* when they are used to link two independent clauses. Example:

> Two of our guns need tube changes; however, we can still use them for direct fire if we must.

2. You may use a semicolon to link two independent clauses. Example:

> The new surgeon has a good preventive medicine program; he developed it without any guidance from higher headquarters.

3. You must use a semicolon to separate series items internally punctuated with commas. Example:

> The commander's itinerary included stops in Brussels, Belgium; Geneva, Switzerland; and Charleston, South Carolina.

4. You must not use a semicolon to introduce quoted material; instead use a colon or a comma.

series. A series is a group of related words or phrases. Separate each element of a series with a comma. Go ahead and put a comma between the next-to-last element and the word connecting it to the last element. If a series is internally punctuated, separate its elements with semicolons. Examples:

> The navigator had her charts, itinerary, and initial headings.

> Many sailors own homes in Norfolk, Virginia; Groton, Connecticut; and Charleston, South Carolina.

set, sit. You can avoid confusing these words if you will remember that *set* means put or place and sit means rest the body on the buttocks. Compare:

> Specialist Meyers must *set* two hundred bricks on the stoop before he may *sit* down and rest.

sexist language. Any use of language that denigrates or discriminates against either sex is sexist. Most examples of sexist language in English are offensive. When you can eliminate sexist language without creating ridiculously awkward constructions, by all means do. One easy way to do this is to use plurals. For example:

Sexist.	A *soldier* must keep *his* rifle clean.
Nonsexist.	A *soldier* must keep *his* or *her* rifle clean.
Better.	*Soldiers* must keep *their* rifles clean.

Sometimes you won't be able to use plural forms. In those cases, select the singular pronoun that seems least likely to offend your readers, and get on with your writing. Do not do this sort of thing:

Awkward.	The *driver* must fill *his/her* vehicle with diesel before *he/she* may pick up *his/her* trip ticket.

Instead, try this:

Better.	The *driver* must fill *her* vehicle with diesel before *she* may pick up a trip ticket.

Or this:

Best.	*Drivers* must fill *their* vehicles with diesel before they may pick up trip tickets.

One thing you can certainly do is eliminate potentially insulting phrases from your writing (and speech). Phrases like *boss woman, old lady, weaker sex,* etc., have no place in military prose.

shall, will. You probably can't please everyone in your use of these two words, but you may come pretty close if you follow this guidance: Avoid using *shall* with any but the first person. Examples:

> *I shall* call.

> *You will* call.

> *Shall I* call?

> *Will you* call?

simple sentence. Chapter 7 deals at some length with the simple sentence. Here, suffice it to say that a simple sentence needs only four things to be a sentence: a capital letter at its beginning, a subject, a verb, and a terminal punctuation mark. If the subject of a sentence is understood, as it often is in the imperative mood, a simple sentence can be one word long. "Stop!" That's a simple sentence. Most simple sentences will have at least two words, though.

site, cite. These words cannot be confused if you remember that *site* is a noun meaning a place or location, and *cite* is a verb meaning to refer to or quote. Compare:

> Specialist Bartleby *cited* the regulation as a basis for limiting entry to the forward *site*.

slow, slowly. Though both these words are adverbs, *slow* is also an adjective and a verb. Of the two adverb forms, *slowly* is the more formal. Opt for *slowly* the adverb and *slow* the adjective, and you will rarely misuse either word. Examples:

> **Adjective.**   The duty officer logged a *slow* night.

> **Adverb.**   He drove *slowly* to the ammunition dump.

> **Verb.**   Three tank barriers *slowed* the company's advance.

split infinitives. Inexperienced editors tend to go berserk when they spot a split infinitive because it's the only usage error they recognize by name. To quickly split an infinitive (as I have just done) requires only that the writer put an adverb or adverbial element between the word *to* and the verb.

Generally, you should not split infinitives. If, however, not splitting an infinitive forces you into a grossly awkward construction, go ahead and split it. A split infinitive will do far less to slow the reading of your work than an awkward presentation will. Go for the lesser evil.

When you have a choice, though, don't split infinitives.

subject. In a sentence written in the active voice, the subject is the word or phrase that performs the action expressed by the verb; in the passive voice, the subject receives the action expressed by the verb.

The person (first, second, or third) and number (singular or plural) of the verb depend on the subject. Singular subjects take singular verbs; plural subjects take plural verbs.

Make it a practice to put the subject as close to the verb as you can. The farther the subject from the verb, the greater the reader's chance of getting lost. And the greater your chances of making an agreement error.

subjective complement. Predicate nominatives and predicate adjectives function as subjective complements of linking verbs. Without a subjective complement, a sentence with a linking verb has virtually no meaning. Examples:

Uncomplemented.	Captain Jacques is.
Predicate nominative.	Captain Jacques is *a very good pilot.*
Uncomplemented.	The three sailors seemed.
Predicate adjective.	The three sailors seemed *unduly anxious.*

subjunctive mood. One of three verbal moods, the subjunctive is primarily used to express conditions that are wished for or hypothetical but generally not possible. For example:

If I *were* you, I *would* go on leave.

The subjunctive mood is not used so freely today as it was fifty years ago. In modern English, it still implies a degree of formality.

Some subjunctive constructions left over from an earlier time serve as convenient ways to begin sentences. *Be that as it may, suffice it to say,* and *far be it from me* are all subjunctive forms. They have their place as useful stylistic devices. In the main, though, they really shouldn't turn up in military writing very often, because they take extra time to read.

subordinating conjunctions. The function of a subordinating conjunction is to connect a subordinate clause to a main clause. Words like *as, because, how, if, since,* and *so* can be subordinating conjunctions. The most common ones—*that, what, where, which,* and *who*—are the words that introduce relative clauses.

subordination. Subordination is fundamental to effective style. By carefully subordinating modifiers, even an unpolished writer can save words and focus the reader's attention where it ought to be. You can drift into faulty subordination by writing a series of subordinate clauses, each modifying the clause that precedes it. Keep your sentences relatively short, and you won't have that problem. On the other hand, if your sentences are too short to allow any subordination, you wind up wasting words. Compare these examples of subordination:

Ineffective.   The meeting was conducted by the command group. They directed that additional emphasis be given to materiel readiness.

Effective.   The command group met, directing additional emphasis on materiel readiness.

Ineffective.   Captain Baryon intended to be present at the meeting he had promised to attend but was unable to because of an urgent telephone call he received as he started toward the conference.

Effective.   Despite his promise to attend, an urgent telephone call made Captain Baryon miss the meeting.

Notice that the rewritten versions of both examples of ineffective subordination save words and focus the reader's attention in an orderly way on the material at issue.

summary. The ability to compose an effective summary will distinguish you from many writers. It will also save you a lot of words; and, as you search for the bottom line of the piece you're summarizing, you will become more critical of your own writing. For the sake of brevity, a summary is superior to either paraphrase or direct quotation. Obviously, you may be exchanging detail for brevity. Decide which is more important for that particular document, then proceed accordingly.

syllabification. The process of dividing a word into its different syllables is called syllabification. When you divide words, make sure you actually divide them between syllables. If you don't know what the syllables are— e.g., is it bot-tle, bott-le, or bo-ttle?—go to the dictionary. There you will find the correct syllabification.

tense. In English there are six verb tenses: three simple (present, past, and future) and three perfect (perfect, past perfect, and future perfect). Here are there uses:

1. The **present tense** expresses things that happen now, things that will happen, and things that always happen. Examples:

Fifteen more soldiers *are becoming* rangers today.

Twenty more *become* rangers tomorrow.

Hundreds *become* rangers each year.

2. The **past tense** expresses things that happened in the past. Example:

Fifteen other soldiers *became* rangers yesterday.

3. The **future tense** expresses things that are going to happen. This tense requires you to use the auxiliary verbs *shall* and *will* as well as the main verb. Avoid using *shall* except in the first person. Examples:

I *shall become* a ranger tomorrow.

Fifteen more soldiers *will become* rangers tomorrow.

4. The **present perfect tense** expresses something that began in the past and continues in the present. Use some form of the verb *to have* with the main verb. Example:

> These fifteen soldiers *have trained* as rangers for nearly nine weeks.

5. The **past perfect tense** expresses something that happened in the past before some other past action or event. Use the auxiliary verb *had* with the main verb. Example:

> Those twenty soldiers *had trained* as rangers for nine weeks before they finally received their ranger tabs.

6. The **future perfect tense** expresses things that will happen in the future but at two different times. Use the auxiliary verbs *will* and *shall,* some form of the verb *to have,* and the main verb to form this tense. Examples:

> Nine weeks *will have passed* before the fifteen soldiers receive their ranger tabs.

> Nine weeks *will have passed* before the fifteen soldiers will receive their ranger tabs.

Note that by using the present form *(receive)* to express the future form *(will receive)* you can save a word.

In addition to those six tenses, you can use the auxiliary verbs *to be* and *to have* to form progressive tenses (e.g., *he had been eating* vs. *he ate, he is eating* vs. *he eats,* etc.). Unless you really need the sense of progression this form conveys, don't use it. For instance, in a sentence like this:

> The generator *is* finally *running.*

you use the progressive form to imply that getting the generator to run at all has been tough. But you might not need it in a sentence like this:

> The generator *is running* every day.

when all you want to say is this:

> The generator *runs* every day.

When you have a choice, save the words.

than, then. Normally used to make comparisons, the conjunction *than* implies an inequitable distinction. *Then,* on the other hand, is an adverb meaning at a particular time, besides, accordingly, or yet. Don't confuse these two words. Compare:

If our troops are tougher *than* theirs, *then* we will win.

that, which. When used to tell or explain something about something else, *that* and *which* function in different ways and, thus, are not interchangeable. *That* restricts to the extent that it identifies; it provides essential information. *Which,* on the other hand, provides nice-to-know information of an explanatory and nonrestrictive sort. The nice-to-know information is set off inside commas, but the essential information is not. Compare these examples:

Restrictive.	The map *that* Commander Christian gave to Mr. Cook is on the bridge.
Nonrestrictive.	The map, *which* Commander Christian gave to Mr. Cook, is on the bridge.
Restrictive.	The quadrant *that* Chief Boggs got calibrated still carried a ten-mil error.
Nonrestrictive.	The quadrant, *which* Chief Boggs got calibrated, still carried a ten-mil error.

there is, there are. These phrases often serve as introductory elements of sentences. In using them, be careful to avoid agreement errors and unnecessarily awkward constructions, particularly if you follow them with collective nouns. Examples:

Wrong.	There *is* a lot of poor *marksmen* on this range.
Right.	There *are* a lot of poor *marksmen* on this range.
Right.	There *is* a lot of *confusion* over this new regulation.

though, although. Both these words mean the same thing. *Though* is slightly less formal than *although*. Choose the word that sounds best for the context you want to use it in. Examples:

> The platoon stumbled into position, *though* the point man had been hopelessly lost.

> *Although* the point man had been hopelessly lost, the platoon stumbled into position.

titles. Most military writers put titles in the wrong format. Here are the rules:

  1. Put the titles of essays, articles, stories, songs, marches, and similar short works in quotation marks.
  2. Put the titles of books, plays, films, and other major works in italics.

Note: When writing by hand or typing, show italics by underlining.

toward, towards. Both of these words mean the same thing. You will be equally correct in using either, but *toward* is more current in American usage.

transitive verbs. A verb that takes an object is a transitive verb. Intransitive verbs do not take an object. Some verbs, depending on the sense you use them in, can be both transitive and intransitive. For example:

> **Intransitive.**   On the rifle range Private Fiero *qualified* easily.

> **Transitive.**   He then *qualified* three other *soldiers*.

truncated verbal adjectives and verbs. There is a tendency in spoken English to omit (or pronounce unclearly) the past-tense endings on certain verbal adjectives and verbs. Some of these words are in pretty common usage. If you want to include them in your writing, be sure you do so correctly. These examples should help:

> **Wrong.**   The trial counsel would have done better, but her mannerisms *prejudice* the court against her.

Right.   The trial counsel would have done better, but her mannerisms *prejudiced* the court against her.

Wrong.   In your dealings with any sailor, it is wrong to be *bias.*

Right.   In your dealings with any sailor, it is wrong to be *biased.*

Wrong.   Specialist Roberts was *suppose* to be at his post, but he failed to appear.

Right.   Specialist Roberts was *supposed* to be at his post, but he failed to appear.

Wrong.   Airman Castor *use* to be quite a daredevil.

Right.   Airman Castor *used* to be quite a daredevil.

Caution: One thing that might complicate your usage of some of these words is their dual nature. *Prejudice* and *bias,* for instance, are verbs, but they are nouns as well. You can use them correctly if you pay attention to the grammatical role you want them to play in what you write. Compare these examples:

Verb.   The trial counsel would have done better, but her mannerisms *prejudiced* the court against her.

Noun.   The trial counsel would have done better but for the *prejudice* her mannerisms created.

Verb.   The unhappy sailor, who knew Commander Albright from another billet, *biased* his shipmates against the new executive officer.

Noun.   By promoting that kind of *bias* before Commander Albright came aboard ship, Seaman Huffer damaged the crew's moral.

uninterested, disinterested. These words are frequently misused. *Uninterested* means indifferent or unconcerned; *disinterested* means objective or impartial. Compare:

General Burgon left early because he was *uninterested* in the second half of the presentation.

As a *disinterested* evaluator, General Burgon listened to the entire presentation before making any kind of judgment.

verbs. Verbs are the words we use to express action. They are also the words that show the relationship between subject and object. The strength and effectiveness of your writing are, in large measure, a function of the strength and effectiveness of your verbs.

Choose your verbs carefully. Select words that will directly and economically transmit the meaning you want to convey. After picking your verbs, use them in the active voice. Avoid using progressive tenses if you can. Keep adverbs to a minimum by choosing precise verbs (i.e., instead of *walked slowly* try *ambled* or *strolled*). And make it a point to use forms of the verb *to be* as infrequently as you can.

voice. Voice shows the nature of the relationship of the subject and the verb. The active voice shows that the subject is responsible for the action expressed by the verb. The passive voice, on the other hand, shows that the subject is (passively) receiving the action. Examples:

Active voice. The shore patrol questioned eight marines.

Passive voice. Eight marines were questioned by the shore patrol.

Despite the tradition that puts much of military writing in the passive voice, make every effort to write in the active voice. One way to ensure that you do is to limit severely your use of the verb *to be.* You cannot write in the passive voice without that verb.

well, good. You can avoid misusing these words if you remember that *well* is both an adverb and an adjective. Regard *good* as an adjective only—even though it can sometimes be properly used as an adverb. Examples:

Wrong. Private Bobadil marches *good.*

Right. Private Bobadil marches *well.*

Right. Private Bobadil does a *good* job of marching.

whether, if. Use *whether* when you need to express doubt or an indirect question; use *if* when you want to introduce a condition. Compare:

Doubt.   I doubt *whether* B-6 will start in this cold weather.

Question.   I don't know *whether* B-6 will start in this cold weather.

Condition. *If* B-6 starts, we'll take it on the march.

which. When using this relative pronoun, try hard to leave no doubt as to its antecedent. One of the more vexing errors in its use occurs when a writer attempts to refer to part (or perhaps all) of a related but nevertheless loose grouping. This example illustrates the point:

Wrong.   The first sortie will depart at 1300Z if the ceiling lifts by 1245Z *which* seems unlikely.

What seems unlikely? The ability of the sortie to fly? An improvement in the weather conditions? The point is, your readers don't know. True, they might figure it out in a minute or two, but when that analysis kicks in, the rapid reading is over. Better just to say what you mean:

Right.   The first sortie will depart at 1300Z if the ceiling lifts by 1245Z. I think it will lift.

Right.   The first sortie will depart at 1300Z if the ceiling lifts by 1245Z. I think it will depart on schedule.

which, that. When used to qualify or identify, *which* and *that* perform different functions, so you may not use them interchangeably. *Which* provides nice-to-know, explanatory information: It does not define or restrict its antecedent. It does, however, need to be placed inside commas. *That* restricts its antecedent by identifying or defining it. The defining information does not belong inside commas. Compare these examples:

Nonrestrictive.   A log, *which* Commander Christian misplaced, turned up in the captain's mess.

Restrictive.   A log *that* Commander Christian misplaced turned up in the captain's mess.

Nonrestrictive.	The message, *which* left the first mate puzzled, seemed clear to Seaman Stuart when he recorded it.
Restrictive.	The message *that* left the first mate puzzled seemed clear to Seaman Stuart when he recorded it.

while. A lot of writers use the temporal conjunction *while* as if it meant the same thing as *whereas* or *although*. It doesn't. It means during the time that. If you use *while,* use it correctly. Examples:

Wrong.	*While* the men worked very hard, the position was still poorly fortified at day's end.
Right.	*Although* the men worked very hard, the position was still poorly fortified at day's end.
Right.	*While* the men in Company B rested, the men in Company C continued to move forward.

white, black. These words are sometimes used to make racial distinctions. Unlike the words *Caucasian* and *Asian, white* and *black* should normally not be capitalized.

who, whom. You can always use these relative pronouns correctly if you memorize a couple of things. *Who* is the nominative or subjective case of the pronoun. That's the form it must take when it is functioning as a subject.

Whom is the accusative or objective case. That's the form the pronoun takes when it functions as an object. All you need to know, then, is whether this relative pronoun is functioning as a subject or an object.

Sometimes, though, using these two words absolutely correctly may work against you. If you use *whom* virtually anywhere but immediately after the verb, it seems stuffy. For example:

Whom are you speaking with?

is actually correct; so is

With *whom* are you speaking?

The reason those examples are correct is that the subject of both happens to be *you; whom* is the object of both. General usage, though, accepts this version:

Who are you speaking with?

Bottom line: In using these words, use them correctly insofar as their very correctness does not impede effective communication by causing the reader to do a double take.

will, shall. In the future tenses, use *shall* only in the first-person singular and plural. Use *will* in all three persons, singular and plural. Whether you use *shall* or *will* in the first person is up to you. In some quarters, *shall* is considered slightly more formal.

-wise. The practice of adding *-wise* to words to create new ones is odious. Don't do it. It's gross to write:

The unit looks good *maintenancewise.*

when instead you can write:

The unit has good maintenance.

or:

The unit's maintenance is good.

your, you're. *Your* is a possessive pronoun meaning "of you." The contraction *you're* means "you are." Do not make the grossly ignorant error of confusing those words. Examples:

Wrong.	*Your* a terrible map reader.
Right.	*You're* a terrible map reader.
Wrong.	*You're* range looks like it needs cleaning.
Right.	*Your* range looks like it needs cleaning.

Index

a, usage of, 126
a lot, usage of, 136
a while, usage of, 141
abbreviations, 126–127
    e.g., usage of, 167
    et al., usage of, 168
    etc., usage of, 168
    i.e., usage of, 174
    Ms., usage of, 182
abridged clauses, 127–128
absolute condition, 57
absolute degree, 153–154
absolute phrases, 128
academic writing, 107–108
accept, usage of, 128, 169
active voice, 52–55, 62, 129, 142, 190, 218
adapt, usage of, 129
adjectival clauses, 129–130, 149, 205–206
adjectives, 130–131, 132
    demonstrative, 163
    possessive, 197
adopt, usage of, 129
adverbial clauses, 131, 149–150
adverbs, 131–133
adverbs, conjunctive, 76–77, 158–159
adverse, usage of, 133
affect, usage of, 133–134, 166–167
agreement
    pronoun-antecedent, 82, 134–135, 166, 204–205
    subject-verb, 79–82, 134, 165
all ready, usage of, 136
all right, usage of, 136
all, usage of, 168–169
already, usage of, 136
also, usage of, 136
alternative views, 110–111
although, usage of, 136, 216
alumna, usage of, 136
alumnae, usage of, 136
alumni, usage of, 136

alumnus, usage of, 136
amend, usage of, 136–137, 167–168
among, usage of, 137, 143
amount, usage of, 137
an, usage of, 126
analysis, 109
and, usage of, 137–138
and/or, usage of, 138
antecedent, 82, 138
any, usage of, 138–139
apostrophes, 139–140
appositive, 140
argument, methodology of
    analysis, 109
    evaluation, 111–112
    evidence, 110
    reasoning, 110–111
    research, 108–109
argument, rules of
    alternative views, 110–111
    evaluation of evidence, 111
    reiteration, 112–113
    research, 109
    thesis, 108
as, usage of, 140, 148, 179–180
as/as, usage of, 160
auxiliary verbs, 141
averse, usage of, 133
award citation, 92
awhile, usage of, 141

bad, usage of, 141
badly, usage of, 141
be, usage of, 141–142
because of, usage of, 165
because, usage of, 142
beside, usage of, 142–143
besides, usage of, 142–143
between, usage of, 137, 143
between you and me, usage of, 143
bias, usage of, 217

223

black, usage of, 143, 220

bottom line (conclusion), 46–49, 53, 84, 85–86, 94, 95, 102–103

brackets, 143–144

brainstorming, 43–45, 46–47, 84, 85, 109

briefing, 93–96

but, usage of, 144

c., usage of, 144

ca., usage of, 144

can, usage of, 144–145, 180

can't but, usage of. *See* can't help but, usage of

can't hardly, usage of, 146

can't help but, usage of, 146

capital letters, 146–147

case
    accusative, 147
    genitive, 148, 171
    nominative, 147, 182
    objective, 142, 147
    possessive, 148, 197
    subjective, 142, 147

censor, usage of, 148–149

censure, usage of, 148–149

cite, usage of, 149, 210

clarity
    editing for, 16, 115–119
    writing for, 62

clause, clauses
    abridged, 128
    adjectival, 129–130, 205–206
    adjective, 149
    adverb, 149–150
    adverbial clauses, 131
    conditional, 157–158
    contact, 159
    dependent, 73–75, 79, 149, 164
    independent, 73–75, 76–78, 137, 149
    noun, 149, 184
    relative, 81, 205–206
    subordinate, 149, 212
    unabridged, 128

collective nouns, 81–82, 150–151

colon, 146, 150–151

comma, commas, 140, 151–153
    in compound sentences, 77
    and conjunctive adverbs, 158–159
    serial, 130–131

comma splice, 75–76, 153

communication, effective, 6–7, 24–26, 49

communication, methods of
    face-to-face, 17, 19–20, 87–88
    radio, 17, 18, 20
    telephone, 17, 18, 20, 87–88
    writing, 17, 19, 20

comparative degree, 153–154

comparison of modifiers, 153–154

competence, 16

complement, complements, 155

complement, usage of, 154–155

complements, subjective, 211

complex sentences, 73, 75, 81, 155

compliment, usage of, 154–155

compound predicates, 156

compound sentences, 73, 76–78, 156

compound subjects, 156–157

compound-complex sentences, 73, 78–79, 155–156

comprehension, reading, 22–24

conditional clauses, 157–158

conjunctions
    as, usage of, 140, 179–180
    coordinating, 77–78, 158, 160
    correlative, 160–161, 182, 183
    defined, 76
    subordinating, 142, 158, 212
    temporal, 220

conjunctive adverbs, 76–77, 158–159

consensus of opinion, usage of, 159

contact clauses, 159

continual, usage of, 159

continuous, usage of, 159

contractions, 65–66, 139–140, 159

coordinating conjunctions, 77–78, 158, 160

correctness, 16, 20
    editing for, 119–120
    sentence construction, 73–79, 82
    spelling, 71–73, 82
    subject-verb agreement, 79–82, 165

correlative conjunctions, 160–161, 182, 183

could care less, usage of, 161

could, usage of, 161, 180–181

criteria, usage of, 79–80, 161

criterion, 160

criticism, 7–8

cue cards. *See* talking paper

dangling modifiers, 161–162
dash, 162–163
decision paper, 85, 90–91
degree (comparison), 153–154
demonstrative adjectives, 163
demonstrative pronouns, 163, 201
dependent clauses, 73–75, 79, 149, 164
dialectic, 42–43, 108
direct object (of sentence), 74–75
direct objects, 164, 185–186
directive, 9
discreet, usage of, 164
discrete, usage of, 164
disinterested, usage of, 164, 217–218
dived, usage of, 164
division of words, 164–165
double negatives, 146, 165
double prepositions, 165
dove, usage of, 164
due to, usage of, 165

each other, usage of, 166, 203
each, usage of, 165–166
economy of force, 109
economy of language, 56
editing
    for clarity, 16, 115–119
    for correctness, 16, 119–120
    highlighter, use of, 120–123
    for organization, 123
    rewriting, 123–124
    for style, 121–123
editorial we, 166
effect, usage of, 133–134, 166–167
efficiency, 5–6, 11–12, 49, 72
e.g., usage of, 167
either, usage of, 167
either/or, usage of, 160, 167, 182
ellipsis, 167
elliptical constructions, 148
else, usage of, 167
e-mail, 11–12, 17, 19
emend, usage of, 136–137, 167–168
eminent, usage of, 168, 175
et al., usage of, 168
etc., usage of, 168
euphemisms, 61, 168
evaluation, 111–112
evaluation report narrative, 92

every, usage of, 168–169
evidence, 110
except, usage of, 128, 169
exclamation point, 169

farther, usage of, 169
fewer, usage of, 169
focus, 11–12
foreign words, 170
formats, general
    business letter, 99
    letter of application, 100
    letter of recommendation, 101
    and military writing, 97–99
    resume, 102–105
    social correspondence, 105
formats, military
    award citation, 92
    decision paper, 85, 90–91
    evaluation report narrative, 92
    examples of, 89–92
    executive summary, 89
    general guidelines, 83–84
    general guidelines (list), 88
    information paper, 84–85
    memorandum, 84, 85, 90
    selecting for use, 84–85
    step-by-step approach to, 85–88
    talking paper, 85, 91, 95
former, usage of, 170, 178
fractions, 170
fragments, 170. *See also* sentence fragments
further, usage of, 169
fused sentences, 78, 170–171

genitive case, 148, 171
gerund, 171–172, 195
gerund phrase, 195
gobbledygook, usage of, 172
good, usage of, 172, 218
got, usage of, 172
gotten, usage of, 172

hanged, usage of, 173
Hegel, Georg Wilhelm Friedrich, 42–43
highlighter, use of, 120–123
hopefully, usage of, 173
hung, usage of, 173
hyphen, 164–165, 170, 173–174

hyphenation, 164–165

I, usage of, 53–54, 174
i.e., usage of, 174
if, usage of, 174–175, 219
imminent, usage of, 168, 175
imperative mood, 54, 175
imply, usage of, 175
in to, usage of, 175–176
in, usage of, 175–176
indefinite pronouns, 201
independent clause, 73–75, 76–78, 137, 149
indicative mood, 176
indirect discourse, 176
indirect objects, 177, 185–186
infer, usage of, 175
infinitive, 177–178, 198–200, 210–211
infinitive phrases, 195–196
information paper, 84–85
interrogative pronouns, 178, 201
into, usage of, 175–176
intransitive verbs, 178, 216
irregardless, usage of, 178
italics, 170
it's, usage of, 178
its, usage of, 178
-ize endings, usage of, 61, 178

jargon, 61
judgment, 82

language, economy of, 56
latter, usage of, 170, 178
lay, usage of, 178–179
lead, usage of, 179
led, usage of, 179
less, usage of, 169
letters
    of application, 100
    business, 99
    of recommendation, 101
lie, usage of, 178–179
lighted, usage of, 179
like, usage of, 140, 179–180
linking verbs, 147, 155, 180
lit, usage of, 179

may, usage of, 144–145, 180
media, usage of, 180
memorandum, 8–9, 84, 85, 90

might, usage of, 161, 180–181
modal auxiliaries, 181
modifiers, 181
    dangling, 161–162
    nonrestrictive, 206–207
    restrictive, 206–207
money, usage of, 181
mood
    imperative, 175, 181–182
    indicative, 176, 181–182
    subjunctive, 157–158, 181–182,
      211–212
most, use of, 57
Ms., usage of, 182

neither/nor, usage of, 160–161, 167, 182
nominative case, 182
none, usage of, 182–183
nonrestrictive modifiers, 206–207
nonsexist language, 183
nor, usage of, 183–184
not hardly, usage of, 184
not only/but also, usage of, 160
noun clauses, 149, 184
nouns, 184
    collective, 81–82, 151–152
    used as verbs, 59–60
number, 184–185
number, usage of, 137
numbers, usage of, 185

object (of sentence), 74–75
objects
    direct, 164, 185–186
    indirect, 177, 185–186
    of prepositions, 185–186
on to, usage of, 186
on, usage of, 186
one another, usage of, 166, 203
one of those who, usage of, 187
only, usage of, 187
onto, usage of, 186
or, usage of, 188
oral presentation. *See* briefing
organization, 16, 20
    bottom line (conclusion), 46–49, 84,
      85–86, 94, 95, 102–103
    brainstorming, 36–42, 43–45, 46–47,
      84, 85, 109
    editing for, 123

outlines, use of, 33–35, 45–46, 47
Orwell, George, 61
owing to, usage of, 165

paragraphs, 188
paragraphs, length of, 86–87
parallel construction, 137–138
parallelism, 188–189
paraphrases, 189
parentheses, 189
participial phrases, 195–196
participle, participles, 189–191
    past, 190, 191, 198–200
    present, 129, 190
parts of speech, 191–192
passive voice, 142, 166, 190, 191, 192, 218
    defined, 52
    use of, 51–54
past participle, 190, 191, 198–200
past tense, 192, 198–200
per, usage of, 192
percent, usage of, 193
perfect tenses, 193
period, 193
periodic sentences, 193–194
person, 194
personal pronouns, 53–54, 62–63, 174,
    194–195, 200
phenomena, usage of, 195
phenomenon, usage of, 195
phrasal verbs, 195
phrase, phrases
    absolute, 128
    gerund, 195
    infinitive, 195–196
    participial, 190–191, 195–196
    prepositional, 195–196, 198
    transitional, 56
phrases to avoid, list of, 66–69
please, usage of, 63–65
plurals
    of nouns, 196–197
    subjects, 79–82
    verbs, 79–82
political correctness, 60–61
Politics and the English Language
    (Orwell), 61
possessive adjectives, 197
possessive case, 197
possessive pronouns, 197, 200

possessives, punctuation of, 139, 202
predicate, 197
predicate adjectives, 211
predicate, compound, 156
predicate nominatives, 211
predominant, usage of, 197–198
predominate, usage of, 197–198
prejudice, usage of, 217
prepositional phrase, 195–196, 198
prepositions, 198
    double, 165
    like, usage of, 140, 179–180
present participle, 190
principal, usage of, 198
principle parts of verbs, 198–200
principle, usage of, 198
prior to, usage of, 200
priorities, 11–12
progressive verb forms, 200
pronoun antecedent, 138
pronoun-antecedent agreement, 82,
    134–135, 166, 204–205
pronouns
    and case, 142
    demonstrative, 163, 201
    indefinite, 201
    interrogative, 178, 201
    personal, 62–63, 174, 200
    possessive, 197, 200
    pronouns, 53–54
    reciprocal, 201, 203
    reference of, 204–205
    reflexive, 200, 205
    relative, 200, 205, 206
pronouns, personal, 194–195
protectionism, 8–9
provided, usage of, 201
providing, usage of, 201
punctuation, 201–202
    of abbreviations, 127
    colon, 146, 150–151
    comma, 77, 130–131, 140, 158–159
    commas, 151–153
    dash, 162–163
    ellipsis, 167
    exclamation point, 169
    hyphen, 164–165, 170, 173–174
    parentheses, 189
    period, 193
    of possessives, 202

question mark, 202
quotation marks, 202–203
semicolon, 76–77, 158–159, 208

quality, definition of, 16
quasi-, usage of, 202
question mark, 202
quotation marks, 202–203

raise, usage of, 203
reading comprehension, 22–24
reading level, 116
real, usage of, 203
really, usage of, 203
rear, usage of, 203
reasoning, 110–111
reciprocal pronouns, 201, 203
redundancy, 4–5, 56–57, 159, 203–204
reflexive pronouns, 200, 205
regardless, usage of, 178
regulations, 9
reiteration, 112–113
relative clauses, 81, 205–206, 212
relative pronouns, 200, 205, 206
research, 108–109
restriction, 109
restrictive modifiers, 206–207
resume, 102–105
rewriting, 123–124
rhetorical questions, 207
role-playing, 10–11, 10–11
royal we, 166
run-on sentences, 78, 170–171, 207

semi-, usage of, 207–208
semicolon, 76–77, 158–159, 208
sentence, elements of
    capitalization, 73, 146–147
    object, 74–75
    punctuation, 73, 76
    subject, 73, 74, 75
    verb, 73, 74, 75
sentence errors
    comma splice, 75–76, 153
    fused sentence, 78
    run-on, 78
    sentence fragment, 54, 74, 76
sentence fragment, 54, 74, 76
sentence, sentences
    complete, 73

complex, 73, 75, 81, 155
compound, 73, 76–78, 156
compound-complex, 73, 78–79,
    155–156
declarative, 54
fused, 170–171
periodic, 193–194
rules for construction, 73–79
run-on, 170–171, 207
simple, 73–76, 210
series, 208
set, usage of, 209
sexist language, 209
shall, usage of, 210, 221
simple sentences, 73–76, 210
singular
    subjects, 79–82
    verbs, 79–82
sit, usage of, 209
site, usage of, 149, 210
slow, usage of, 210
slowly, usage of, 210
social correspondence, 105
spelling, 71–73, 82
split infinitive, 177–178, 210–211
style, 16, 20
    active vs. passive constructions, 51–55
    editing for, 121–123
    euphemisms, 61
    -ize endings, usage of, 61
    jargon, 61
    political correctness, 60–61
    sentence variety, 73–79
    tone, 63–66
    vocabulary, 55–62
    voice, 52–55, 62
subject, 211
subjective complements, 211
subjects, compound, 156–157
subject-verb agreement, 79–82, 134, 165
    in complex sentences, 81
    rules of, 79
subjunctive mood, 157–158, 211–212
subordinate clauses, 149
subordinating conjunctions, 142, 158, 212
subordination, 212
substance, 16, 20
    content, 27–28, 45
    defined, 27
    format, 28

knowledge of subject, 31
research, 28–31
mmary, 213
perlative degree, 57, 153–154
llabification, 213

lking paper, 85, 91, 95
mporal conjunctions, 220
nse
  future, 213
  future perfect, 193, 213–215
  past, 129, 192, 213
  past perfect, 193, 213–215
  present, 129, 213
  present perfect, 193, 213–215
an, usage of, 148, 215
ank you, usage of, 63–65
at, usage of, 215, 219–220
en, usage of, 215
ere are, usage of, 215
ere is, usage of, 215
esis, 108
ough, usage of, 136, 216
me, efficient use of, 6, 11–12, 49, 51
tles, 216
ne
  contractions, 65–66
  personal pronouns, 53–54, 62–63
  phrases to avoid, list of, 66–69
  please, usage of, 63–65
  thank you, usage of, 63–65
ward, usage of, 216
wards, usage of, 216
ansitive verbs, 164, 216
uncated verbal adjectives and verbs,
  216–217

ninterested, usage of, 164, 217–218
nity error, 85
sage
  nouns as verbs, 59–60
  verbs as nouns, 57–59

erbal adjectives, truncated, 216–217
erbs, 218
  auxiliary, 141, 181
  intransitive, 178, 216
  irregular, 198–200
  linking, 147, 155, 180
  phrasal, 195

principal parts of, 198–200
progressive, 200
regular, 198
transitive, 164, 216
truncated, 216–217
used as nouns, 57–59
very, use of, 57
vocabulary
  general rules, 56
  military jargon, 61
  redundancy, 159
voice
  active, 52–55, 62, 129, 142, 190, 218
  passive, 52–55, 142, 166, 190, 191, 192,
    218
voice of writer, 10–11

well, usage of, 172, 218
whether, usage of, 174–175, 219
which, usage of, 215, 219–220
while, usage of, 141, 220
white, usage of, 143, 220
who, usage of, 147–148, 220–221, 220–221
whom, usage of, 147–148, 220–221,
  220–221
will, usage of, 210, 221
-wise ending, usage of, 221
writers
  and criticism, 7–8
  and ego, 6–8
  protective instinct of, 8–9
  responsibilities of, 4–6, 16, 20
  rules for, 4–12
  rules for (list), 12–13
writing
  academic, 107–108
  alternatives to, 17–18
  for clarity, 62
  efficiency, 5–6, 72
  e-mail, 11–12, 17, 19
  as the last resort, 19–20, 22–26
  military, standard for, 15–16
  and mission focus, 8–9
  purposes of, 20–22, 41
  redundancy, 4–5, 56–57, 159, 203–204
  for someone else's signature, 10–11, 53,
    65

your, usage of, 221
you're, usage of, 221

STACKPOLE BOOKS

Military Professional Reference Library

Armed Forces Guide to Personal Financial Planning
Air Force Officer's Guide
Airman's Guide
Army Officer's Guide
Army Dictionary and Desk Reference
Career Progression Guide
Combat Service Support Guide
Combat Leader's Field Guide
Enlisted Soldier's Guide
Guide to Effective Military Writing
Guide to Military Operations Other Than War
Job Search: Marketing Your Military Experience
Military Money Guide
NCO Guide
Reservist's Money Guide
Servicemember's Legal Guide
Servicemember's Guide to a College Degree
Today's Military Wife
Veteran's Guide to Benefits
Virtual Combat: A Guide to Distributed Interactive Simulation

Professional Reading Library

Beyond Terror
by Ralph Peters

Roots of Strategy: Books 1, 2, 3, and 4

Guardians of the Republic: A History of the NCO Corps
by Ernest F. Fisher